Storybook CROCHET

Storybook CROCHET

over 25 easy-to-crochet miniature dolls including their costumes and accessories

SALLY ANN GRONSAND

Butterick Publishing

Acknowledgments

Thanks to Julia Porticelli for being in the right place at the right time.

Thanks to Bruce Fitzgerald for infinite patience, kindness, and understanding.

Thanks to Johanna Bafaro for giving me a start and making my hobby my profession.

Thanks to Evelyn Brannon for her enthusiasm and guidance in making a dream become a book.

Thanks to Rosemary Cohen for being.

Photography by Bob Connolly
Illustrations by Phoebe Gaughan
Book Design by Sallie Baldwin

Library of Congress Catalog Card Number: 76-57295
International Standard Book Number: 0-88421-030-8
Copyright © 1977 by Butterick Publishing
161 Sixth Avenue, New York, New York 10013
A Division of American Can Company

To my daughter Christine and my son Frank,
for the love they have given me.

Contents

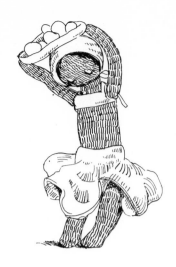

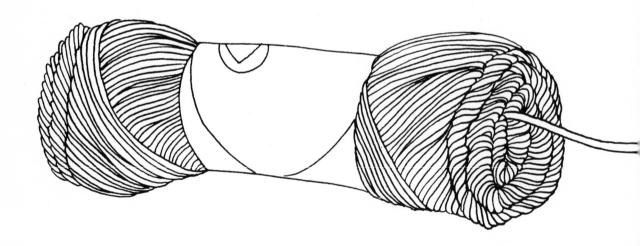

1
Introduction

HOW TO USE
THIS BOOK

Crocheting is a term for creating a fabric with interlocking loops. The word "crochet" comes from the French *croc*, meaning hook, for the interlocking loops of crochet are customarily made with a short hook. Evidence of crochet has been found in various cultures throughout history, including pre-Christian Egypt, ancient China, and among primitive American Indian tribes. Historians have concluded that, since the basic method of crochet is so simple, it has evidently been discovered and rediscovered since the beginning of civilization.

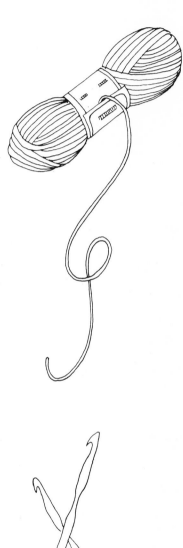

The first actual remnants of early crochet come from middle Europe during the Renaissance when it was used primarily as a form of lace making. Crochet reappeared in the middle of the nineteenth century in England, France, and then Ireland, where it was taught by sympathetic English and European ladies to Irish women who were suffering the disastrous economic results of the potato famine of 1846. When their gift of fine Irish lace was presented to Queen Victoria, crochet came to the attention of English ladies of high fashion. The craft was featured soon after in the American magazine, *Godey's Lady's Book*, where it captured the attention of readers on this side of the Atlantic.

In the past, crochet has been used primarily for trimmings, doilies, tablecloths, and bedspreads, usually in sectional or patchwork form. But, beginning with the crocheted vest craze around 1970, the art of crochet has attracted many new imaginative designers. They have taken this venerable craft and combined it with today's sense of color and limitless variety of textured yarns and made it into a versatile craft with infinite possibilities for creativity and personal satisfaction. Because of its simplicity, endless variety, and portability, crochet has proved to be one of the most popular crafts.

Miniatures, like crochet, have a long history, for small things have intrigued people through the ages. The early Egyptians de-

11

picted aspects of their culture using dolls in displays of miniature scenes showing people at work and play. Almost every subsequent age and culture fashioned miniature figures and objects to reflect their history. We realize the universal appeal of miniatures when we observe an adult spending more time with the model railroad or doll house than the child for whom it was intended. And children naturally relate to small things that they can hold in their hands and play with, sparking their imaginations and fueling their fantasies. The crocheted dolls in this book therefore are for both children and adults.

As you make these delightful and lovable dolls, I'm sure you will find, as I did, that each one will take on a character all its own. Although you will find the instructions simple to follow and the dolls easy to duplicate, none of the faces will look exactly like any other. Your fun and enthusiasm will be heightened by the realization that although the procedures are the same, each doll is unique and different.

I have included a chapter for beginners, Crochet Basics, which contains all the stitches used in this book. With a little practice, you will find your own way of holding the yarn and keeping tension as you work. For these projects you will be working with relatively thin yarn and a small crochet hook. This insures that the stitches are close enough together so that when the dolls are stuffed there will be no gaps for the stuffing to show through. More information about the stitch gauge is explained on page 21.

The cost of materials used in these projects is minimal. Each ball of yarn retails for under a dollar, and more than five separate dolls can be made from one two-ounce skein. The Modern Girl doll and her entire wardrobe can be made for less than the cost of one outfit for a commercial doll. The time it takes to complete an entire project is also minimal. You can construct a finished doll from head to toe in under two hours—with practice, in even less time. You will find increased satisfaction when you have completed and dressed your first little doll in one evening, and for less than two dollars.

These dolls can be far more than just toys. The Dolls With Historical Costumes, for example, make excellent displays for school use, as do the Dolls From Many Lands. Some of the dolls and accessories can be used as table or cake decorations, gift package decorations, and sachets. Many intriguing ideas for using the dolls are included in chapter 9, Dolls, Dolls, and More Dolls. And I have no doubt that they would make very successful fund raisers for church bazaars, flea markets, and craft shows.

After you have made several dolls and their outfits, you will have enough experience with the basic methods of costume construction to begin to think of additional costumes on your own. Storybooks and encyclopedias are an excellent source for new design ideas. Experiment, too, with different hair styles, for although the forms are similar, the variety is endless.

The key to the dolls in this book is the basic doll which is about 5½″ tall on a scale of one inch to one foot. Each costume has been designed to fit this figure. To complement a few of the costumes, I have suggested some simple embroidery. Only four basic stitches are used which are clearly diagramed in the Embroidery Stitch Glossary, page 172.

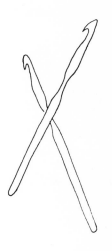

I wish you many happy hours of crocheting these dolls. There is nothing more rewarding than making something with your own two hands. And when that creation is an object that will bring lasting joy to you, your family, and friends, the work takes on a new dimension and is turned, as if by magic, into pleasure.

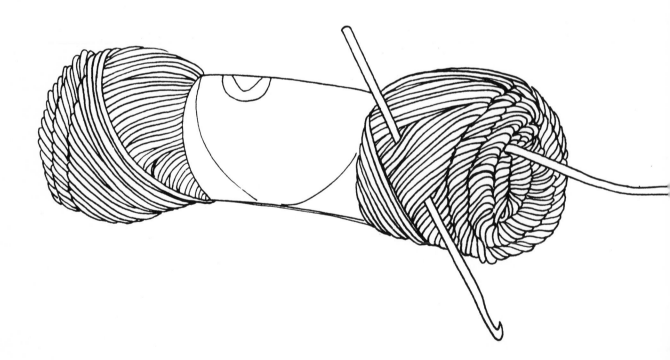

2
Crochet Basics

STITCHES

Slip Knot

The slip knot begins a chain. Using the illustration as a guide, form a circle of yarn and cross it with the yarn attached to the skein. Pull the center yarn through the circle and tighten it on the hook. (Illustration 1)

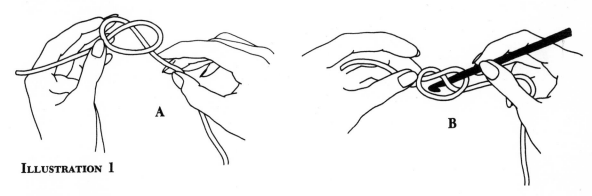

ILLUSTRATION 1

Chain Stitch (ch)

Make a slip knot on the hook (Illustration 2). Holding hook in your right hand, the end of yarn extending from the loop in your left hand and the main length of yarn over the index finger of your left hand, ° place main length over hook, then draw the yarn and hook through the loop (1st stitch). Repeat from ° for the desired number of stitches on your foundation chain. Any pattern may be worked on the foundation chain. (Illustration 3)

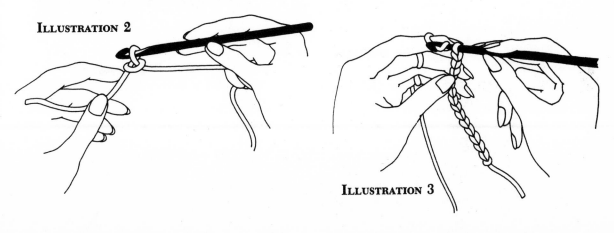

ILLUSTRATION 2

ILLUSTRATION 3

Slip Stitch (sl)

The slip stitch is used to join a round (Illustration 4) or to advance the stitch while skipping a space (Illustration 5). The stitch has no height. Insert hook in stitch, yarn over and draw through stitch and through loop on hook.

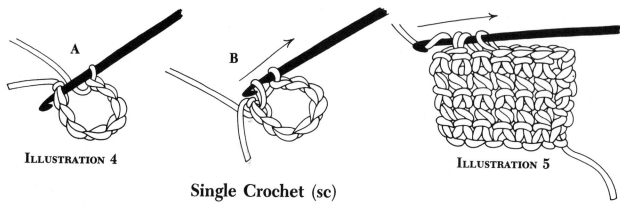

ILLUSTRATION 4

ILLUSTRATION 5

Single Crochet (sc)

Insert hook in 2nd chain from hook, yarn over and pull a loop through the chain. Yarn over again and pull another loop through 2 loops on hook. (Illustration 6)

To increase: Work two stitches in one single stitch. (Illustration 7)

To decrease: Pull a loop through the next stitch and the one after. Then, yarn over and pull loop through the three loops on the hook. (Illustration 8)

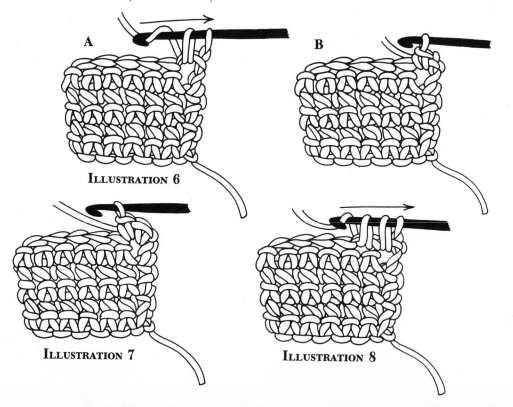

ILLUSTRATION 6

ILLUSTRATION 7

ILLUSTRATION 8

Half Double Crochet (hdc)

Insert hook in 3rd chain from hook, yarn over and pull a loop through the chain. Yarn over and pull yarn through all 3 loops on hook. (Illustration 9)

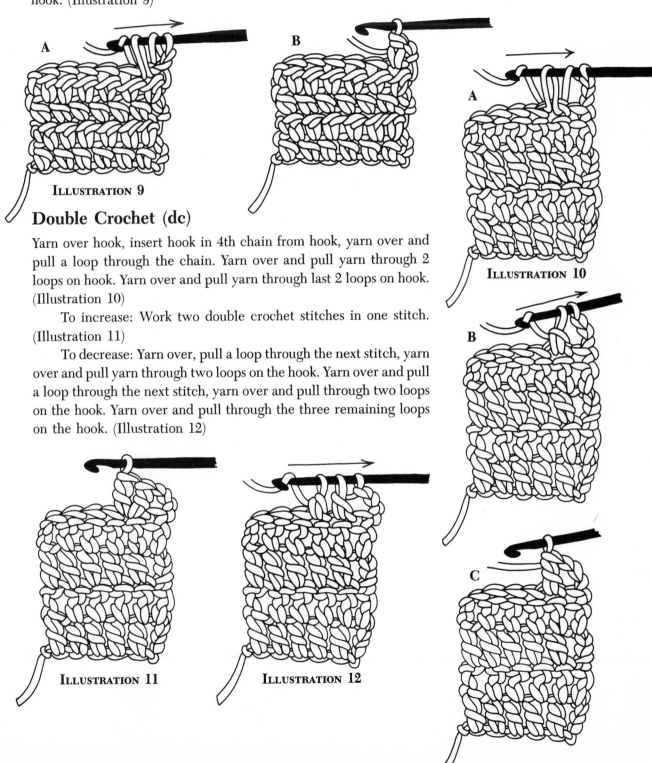

ILLUSTRATION 9

Double Crochet (dc)

Yarn over hook, insert hook in 4th chain from hook, yarn over and pull a loop through the chain. Yarn over and pull yarn through 2 loops on hook. Yarn over and pull yarn through last 2 loops on hook. (Illustration 10)

To increase: Work two double crochet stitches in one stitch. (Illustration 11)

To decrease: Yarn over, pull a loop through the next stitch, yarn over and pull yarn through two loops on the hook. Yarn over and pull a loop through the next stitch, yarn over and pull through two loops on the hook. Yarn over and pull through the three remaining loops on the hook. (Illustration 12)

ILLUSTRATION 10

ILLUSTRATION 11

ILLUSTRATION 12

Triple Crochet (tr)

Work desired number of chain stitches. Yarn over hook twice, insert hook in 5th chain from hook, yarn over and pull a loop through the chain. * yarn over and pull yarn through 2 loops on hook. Repeat from * two more times. (Illustration 13)

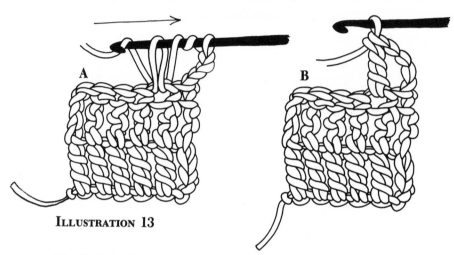

ILLUSTRATION 13

Shell Stitch

The shell stitch is made of several individual stitches repeating in a pattern and fanning out from a single stitch. Many possible stitch combinations will form the shell. Individual directions will specify the stitch pattern to be used. (Illustration 14)

ILLUSTRATION 14

Picot

The picot is a pattern stitch usually used as a decorative edging. It consists of a series of chain stitches and slip stitches repeated in a close pattern to create a series of small points or projections. (Illustration 15)

ILLUSTRATION 15

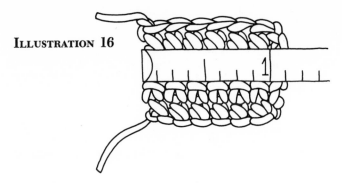

ILLUSTRATION 16

Gauge:

Gauge is an important part of any crochet directions. Gauge instructions look like this: 6 sts   = 1 inch
                              7 rows = 1 inch

Gauge:

> The directions mean that there should be six stitches to a
> horizontal inch of crochet and seven rows to a vertical inch of
> crochet. By keeping the gauge uniform throughout a project, all
> parts will fit together easily. (Illustration 16)

Beginning a New Color

When it is necessary to change yarn color, the instructions will
indicate when the color is to be attached. There are two methods.

Method 1. Pull the new color yarn into the indicated space in
the crochet pattern and tie with a simple knot. Insert the crochet
hook in the same space and pull through a loop. Continue working.
(Illustration 17)

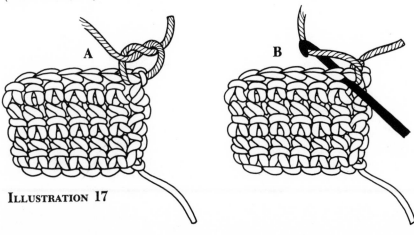

A   B

ILLUSTRATION 17

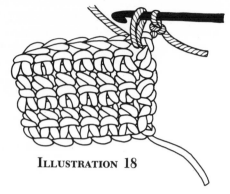

ILLUSTRATION 18

Method 2. Make a slip knot (just as you would to start any chain or project). Put hook through the indicated space in the crochet pattern and pull through a loop. Slip stitch by pulling the loop through the slip knot on the hook. (Illustration 18)

Fastening Off

At the end of the project or a color, the yarn must be secured. To secure, chain-1 and cut for a $\frac{3}{4}''$ yarn end. Pull yarn end through loop. (Illustration 19)

To make a neat finish, use the crochet hook to weave the yarn end underneath the stitches on the back of the work. (Illustration 20)

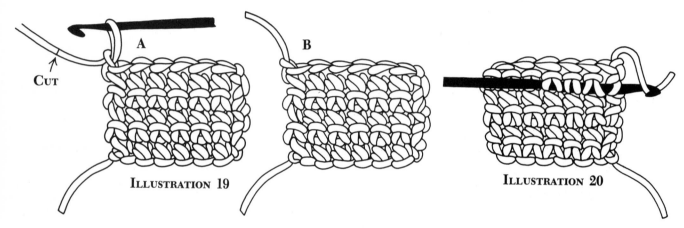

ILLUSTRATION 19   **ILLUSTRATION 20**

Putting Motifs Together

One way to join crochet is sewing. Place edges adjacent to each other. With a tapestry needle and yarn (or a sewing needle and thread), pick up one yarn in each stitch and whip stitch the edges together. Secure yarn at the beginning and end with back stitches. (Illustration 21)

Another way is to slip stitch the edges together. Attach a piece

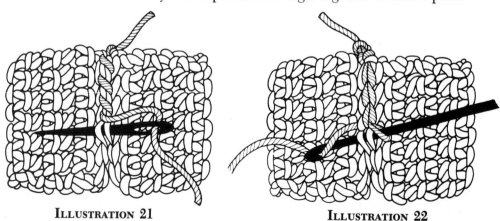

ILLUSTRATION 21   **ILLUSTRATION 22**

of yarn. With the crochet hook pull a loop through a single stitch in each edge. Slip stitch and continue to join edges in the same way. Fasten off. (Illustration 22)

Pompom

Cut two cardboard donuts using the drawing as a size guide. Put the two cards together and wrap with yarn until center hole is filled and cardboard is covered. Cut the yarn all around by cutting between the two circles. Tie tightly between cardboard circles. Remove cardboard circles and trim ball evenly. (Illustration 23)

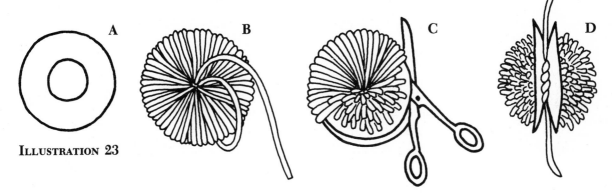

ILLUSTRATION 23

Fringe:

Use a strip of cardboard as wide as the desired length of the fringe. Wrap yarn around the cardboard evenly. Cut through yarn on one side of the wrapped cardboard. Each yarn piece will be twice the finished length of the fringe. Fold in half and use a crochet hook to draw fold through the edge. Pull the yarn ends through the loop and pull tight. (Illustration 24)

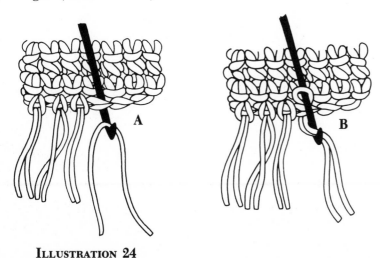

ILLUSTRATION 24

MATERIALS

The materials used in this book are simple and easy to find. For the photographed dolls I have used Coats & Clark's Sock & Sweater Yarn almost exclusively. This yarn comes in a wide variety of colors and is nationally distributed through craft and variety stores. It is colorfast, machine washable and dryable. The embroidery floss used on photographed dolls and costumes is J. P. Coats, available in most fabric and variety stores. Whatever brand of yarn or embroidery floss you use, the results will be the same, providing the gauge is the same. Keep in mind that Sock & Sweater Yarn is thin, similar to fingering yarn. White angora yarn was used as trim for several costumes, including the Princess's cape, and for the Bunny. Two ten-gram balls of angora will suffice to make every item in the book that calls for it.

The crochet hook used throughout—with only a few exceptions, noted in the individual set of instructions—is a size #2 steel crochet hook. Using sock and sweater yarn and the #2 hook, the gauge is 6 stitches to 1 inch, 7 rows to 1 inch.

In addition, you will need a sewing needle, mercerized cotton thread for sewing, a size #18 tapestry needle, size 000 snaps, and polyester fiberfill. Polyester fiberfill is a soft, washable, hypoallergenic stuffing. It comes in a 16-ounce package at variety and fabric stores. It costs under two dollars and contains more than enough filling for every item in the book.

Before starting any of the projects, please read the Helpful Hints section. Then, select the doll or accessory of your choice, gather your materials and equipment together, and begin. Never forget that the most important ingredients for a successful project are your own two hands.

ABBREVIATIONS

st   stitch
sts   stitches
ch   chain
sc   single crochet
hdc   half double crochet
dc   double crochet
tr   triple crochet
sk   skip
sl   slip
rnd   round
inc   increase
dec   decrease
tog   together
yo   yarn over
beg   beginning
bet   between
ea   each
*   repeat instructions following the asterisk as many times as specified.

HELPFUL HINTS

- Since most of the items in this book are small, when ending off, leave the yarn end about ½ to ¾ inch long. With your crochet hook, weave the ends in and out until secure; then trim.

- When working in straight single crochet, there is usually a *ch 1, turn* at the end of the row. When starting the next row, work right into the first stitch. When working in double crochet, there is usually a *ch 3, turn* at the end of the row. When starting the next row, work into the second stitch as the ch 3 counts as the first stitch. Work the last stitch of the row into the top of the ch 3 of the row below.

- The arms and legs of the dolls and animals are small tubelike pieces, worked in rounds. This may seem a bit awkward at first, but once you have worked the first couple of rounds, they go easily. Make sure when you start that the chain is not twisted when joined. And check when the first round is completed that you have the proper number of stitches. As you work the rounds, take care not to catch the stitches on the other side of the tube.

- When working any item which is done in rounds, a marker should be placed at the end of the first round. Use a piece of yarn about an inch long and place it between the first and last stitch of the round. When the item is finished you can just slip it out. The marker is almost essential when working in rounds as it will help you keep an accurate count for each round. (Illustration 25)

ILLUSTRATION 25

- In order for the objects to come out exactly to scale, it is a good idea to check your count or gauge at the end of each row. This insures that the dolls will be uniform in size and that the clothes will fit perfectly.

- Baby yarn or its equivalent, sock and sweater yarn, is used throughout, unless otherwise indicated. It is important to use the weight of yarn called for in each pattern as a substitute will alter the size. Fingering yarn works up slightly smaller in gauge than baby yarn. If another yarn is used for the doll, such as sport weight, make sure to use that same weight for the costume.

- When putting a finishing row of single crochet around the outer edge of a garment and turning a corner, be sure to make the last single crochet of one edge and the first single crochet of the next in the same space with a ch 1 in between. When putting a finishing edge along the side of a garment, make 1 single crochet in each row. If you are making a double crochet edging, put 2 single crochets in each row.

- As you attach the yarn to begin an edging, leave an end about 1 inch long; hold it along the edge of the garment and work stitches over the loose end to secure it.

- When snaps are called for in a materials list, they are sewn on to the finished garment for closure.

- The needle used in the projects are sewing needles, embroidery needles, and tapestry needles. Use sewing needles with thread to assemble dolls, sew on snaps, and assemble costumes. Use embroidery needles and embroidery floss for adding decorative touches to the garments. Use tapestry needles for adding hair to the dolls.

3
The Doll

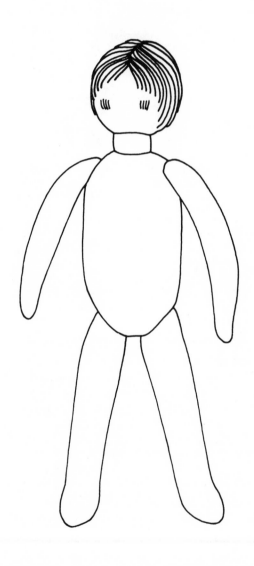

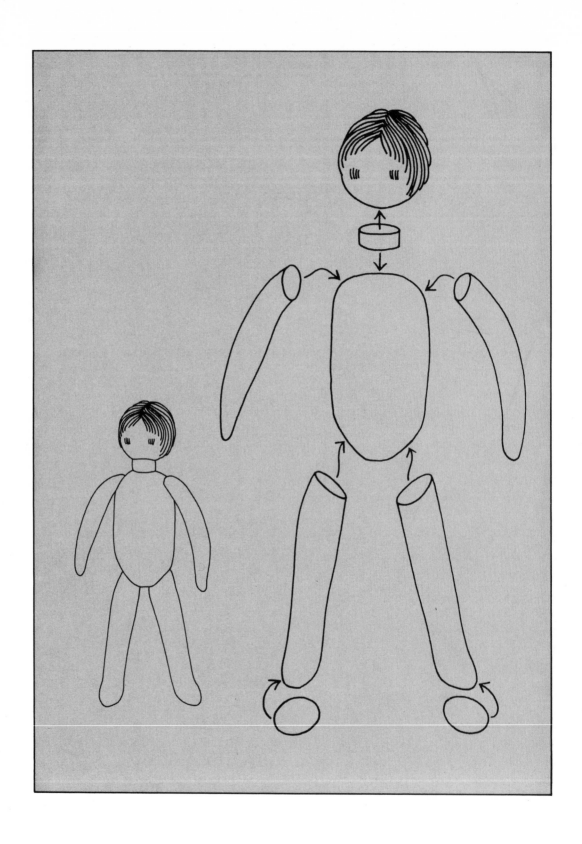

CONSTRUCTION

The construction of the basic doll is the key to this book. Once you have mastered it, you will want to make each and every doll given here. It takes so little time to make a single doll that making one for practice is a good investment in time and experience.

Materials:
>   Sock and sweater yarn in pink and black
>   Steel crochet hook, size #2
>   Polyester fiberfill
>   Pink mercerized cotton thread
>   Embroidery floss in black

Gauge:
>   6 sts = 1 inch
>   7 rows = 1 inch

HEAD

With pink yarn, ch 4, sl to 1st ch to form ring.

Rnd 1: 6 sc in center of ring. Place marker to indicate beg of rnd.

Rnd 2: 2 sc in ea st (12 sc).

Rnd 3: ° 1 sc in next st, 2 sc in next st °. Repeat bet ° to end of rnd (18 sc).

Rnd 4: ° 1 sc in next 2 sts, 2 sc in next st °. Repeat bet ° to end of rnd (24 sc).

Rnd 5: Work even on 24 sc until 9 rnds complete.

Rnd 10: ° 1 sc in next 2 sts [insert hook into next st and pull yarn through; keeping yarn on hook, insert hook into next st, yo hook and through all 3 loops (dec made)] °. Repeat bet ° to end of rnd.

Rnd 11: ° 1 sc in next st, dec next 2 sts °. Repeat bet ° to end of rnd.

Stuffing

Insert fiberfill through opening, stuffing firmly to make head as round as possible. Finish head by working dec until opening is completely closed. End off. Weave end through and trim.

NECK
Ch 10, sl to 1st ch to form ring.
Rnd 1: 1 sc in ea st (10 sc). Work even until 3 rnds complete. End off.

BODY
Work the same as head for 1st 4 rnds. Work even on 24 sc until 15 rnds complete.
Rnd 16: Same as Rnd 10 of head.
Rnd 17: Same as Rnd 11 of head.

Stuffing
Insert fiberfill through opening, stuffing firmly to mold into a body shape. Finish body by working dec until opening is completely closed. End off by cutting yarn and pulling through last st. Weave end through and trim.

ARMS
Ch 8, sl to 1st ch to form ring.
Rnd 1: 1 sc in ea st of ch (8 sc).
Rnd 2: Work 1 sc in ea st and continue until 14 rnds complete.
Rnd 15: Work dec until completely closed. Pull yarn through last loop. Secure and pull end to the inside by reaching hook through opening, catching yarn, and pulling it to the inside. Make two arms.

Stuffing
Stuff arms loosely, using small pieces of fiberfill and poking them through opening with heavy end of crochet hook.

LEGS
Ch 10, sl to 1st ch to form ring.
Rnd 1: 1 sc in ea st (10 sc). Continue to work even on 10 sc until 15 rnds complete. Make two legs.

Feet
Row 16: Work 5 sc, ch 1, turn.
Row 17: 1 sc in 2nd st, 1 sc in next 3 sts, ch 1, turn.
Row 18: 1 sc in 2nd st, 1 sc in next 2 sts. End off. Make two feet.

Soles
Ch 4, sl to 1st ch to form ring.
Rnd 1: 6 sc in center of ring. Place marker to indicate beg of rnd.

32

Rnd 2: 3 sc in next st, 2 sc in next 2 sts, 3 sc in next st, 2 sc in next 2 sts, sl 1 st. End off. Make two soles.

Assembling

Pin sole to bottom of foot flap. Work sl st, attaching edge of foot to sole piece. Or sew sole to bottom of foot. See Illustration 26(a).

Stuffing

Insert small pieces of fiberfill through opening. Work stuffing into foot with heavy end of crochet hook. Unlike arms, make the legs firm.

SEWING

Use pink mercerized cotton thread double. Pin the neck to the bottom of the head and sew on. See Illustration 26(b). It is easier to embroider the eyes and add the hair before continuing the total construction. With black embroidery floss, sew the eyes about 3 rnds up from the neck with about 5 sc in between. You can start the floss or yarn up through the neck opening and end it the same way. Satin stitch on 1 sc about three or four times for each eye.

HAIR

Use either black yarn or embroidery floss double using all 6 strands. You can draw a line from the forehead straight back for a guide, as shown in frontview. Insert needle at A and out through B. Continue working as shown in sideview. Work right side, then left side to correspond. Finish working back of head. The stitches should come from the center top of head to the base of the head at the top of the neck, as shown in backview. (Illustration 27)

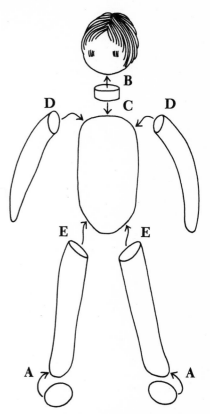

ILLUSTRATION 26

ILLUSTRATION 27

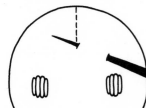
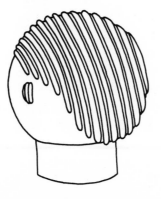

FRONT   **SIDE**   **BACK**

All hairdos are made in the same manner. Pigtails, ponytails, and buns are added for various styles and are explained in the instructions for each doll. These extra features for hair styling can be added after the rest of the doll has been finished.

ASSEMBLING

When the head is finished completely, place a very small amount of stuffing in the neck opening. Next sew the body to the bottom of the neck, making sure the tapered end is at the bottom. See Illustration 26(c). Sew the arms 2 rnds below the neck directly in line with sides (d). Sew the legs to bottom of body directly in line with sides, fitting the tapered end to the body (e). Sew each section to the other firmly, using double thread and making small whip stitches.

4
Dolls with Historical Costumes

The Dolls with Historical Costumes cover a range of typical American dress from colonial times to the present day.

Let this section stimulate your imagination as you begin to think of your own ideas for costumes. Change the colors, the length of a gown, and add your own innovative touches of crochet trim embroidery. Try different textures of yarn and mix your stitches. A few experiments can expand the wardrobe of any doll you choose.

The Early American costumes for both the boy and girl are representative of the clothing worn by the Pilgrim settlers around 1620. The dolls are named Priscilla and John.

The Southern Belle's dress, including her straw bonnet, is typical of the clothing worn in the mid-19th century. This Southern beauty is named Scarlett.

The next doll is Flora the Flapper, who represents the lively era of the 1920s with her jaunty dress and cloche hat.

Today's Modern Girl has a memorable wardrobe of blue jeans and sweater, camel's-hair coat trimmed in fur with matching fur beret, and a sunny yellow dress and wide-brimmed hat. This thoroughly modern gal is called Kelly.

PRISCILLA THE PILGRIM GIRL

COLOR PLATE 1

Make the basic doll.
Hair style/Regular with gold embroidery floss

Costume/Dress, Collar, Apron, and Hat

Materials:
    Sock and sweater yarn in black and white
    Steel crochet hook, size #2
    Snaps, size 000
    Black and white mercerized cotton thread
Gauge:
    6 sts = 1 inch
    7 rows = 1 inch

DRESS
With black yarn, ch 18.
Row 1: 1 sc in 2nd ch from hook, 1 sc in ea st of ch (16 sc), ch 1, turn.
Row 2: 2 sc in ea st across (32 c), ch 1, turn.
Row 3: 1 sc in next 5 sts, ch 5, sk 5 sts, 1 sc in next 12 sts, ch 5, sk 5 sts, ch 1, turn.
Row 4: 1 sc in ea st across, picking up 5 sc in ea ch 5, ch 1, turn.
Row 5: 1 sc in ea st across (32 sc), ch 1, turn.
Repeat Row 5 until 10 rows complete. Ch 3, turn.
Row 11: (Ch 3 counts as 1st dc), 2 dc in 2nd st and ea st across, ending 1 dc in last st, ch 3, turn.
Row 12: 1 dc in ea st across (62 dc), ch 3, turn.
Repeat Row 12 seven more times. End off.
Sew up back seam to just below waist. Close at neck with snaps.

Sleeves

Attach yarn at underarm sleeve opening. Pick up 12 sc evenly spaced. Work 11 rnds even. End off. Make two sleeves.

Cuffs

Attach white yarn at sleeve edge and work 4 rnds even. End off. Fold cuffs back. Make two cuffs.

COLLAR

With white yarn, ch 16.

Row 1: 1 sc in 2nd ch from hook and ea st of ch (15 sc), ch 1, turn.

Row 2: 1 sc in 1st st, 2 sc in next 6 sts, 3 sc in next st, 2 sc in next 6 sts, 1 sc in last st, ch 1, turn (29 sc).

Row 3: 1 sc in next 14 sts, 3 sc in next st, 1 sc in last 14 sts, turn.

Row 4: Sl 1st 7 sts, 1 sc in next 7 sts, 3 sc in next st, 1 sc in next 7 sts, sl 1 st, turn.

Row 5: Sl 5 sts, 1 sc in next 3 sts, 3 sc in next st, 1 sc in next 3 sts, sl 1 st. End off.

Attach yarn to the outer edge at opening and make 1 row of sc around entire outer edge to finish. Close at back with snaps.

APRON

With white yarn, ch 19.

Row 1: 1 sc in 2nd ch from hook and ea st of ch (18 sc), ch 3, turn.

Row 2: (Ch 3 counts as 1st dc), 1 dc in ea st, ch 1, turn.

Row 3: 1 sc in ea st across row, ch 3, turn.

Row 4: Repeat Rows 2 and 3, four more times.

Tie

Ch 20, attach to right corner of last row worked. Pick up a loop in next 3 sts (4 loops on hook), pull yarn through all 4 loops. Repeat four more times, 1 sc in last st, ch 20. End off. Attach yarn to upper left corner and work 1 row sc to finish off edge.

HAT

With white yarn, ch 22.

Row 1: 1 sc in 2nd ch from hook, 1 sc in ea st of ch (21 sc), ch 1, turn.

Row 2: Sk 1st 2 sts, 1 sc in 3rd st and ea st across (19 sc), ch 1, turn. Repeat Row 2 six more times. This will automatically reduce 1 st ea row.

ILLUSTRATION 28

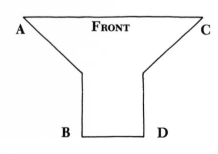

40

Row 9: Working even on 8 sts, 1 sc in ea st, ch 1, turn, for 8 rows. End off.

Sew A to B, C to D. When sides are sewn together, starting at center back, right side facing you, work 1 row of sc around edge to finish off. (Illustration 28)

JOHN THE PILGRIM BOY

COLOR PLATE 1

Make the **basic doll** except crochet the legs with white yarn. Follow the basic leg pattern up to round 14. End off. Attach black yarn and work 1 rnd even. Row 16: Work 5 sc, ch 1, turn. Row 17: 1 sc in 2nd st, 1 sc in next 2 sts. End off. Make sole in black as in basic doll. Sew sole to foot or sl st tog in black.

Hair style/Regular with orange embroidery floss.

Costume/Jacket, Pants, Collar, and Hat

Materials:
    Sock and sweater yarn in black and white
    Steel crochet hook, size #2
    Snaps, size 000
    Black mercerized cotton thread
Gauge:
    6 sts = 1 inch
    7 rows = 1 inch

41

JACKET

With black yarn, ch 17.

Row 1: 1 sc in 2nd ch from hook and ea st of ch (16 sc), ch 1, turn.

Row 2: 2 sc in ea st across (32 sc), ch 1, turn.

Row 3: 1 sc in 1st 6 sts, ch 5, sk 5 sts, 1 sc in next 10 sts, ch 5, sk 5 sts, 1 sc in last 6 sts, ch 1, turn.

Row 4: 1 sc in ea st across, picking up 5 sc in ea ch 5, ch 1, turn.

Row 5: Work even on 32 sc, ch 1, turn, for 9 more rows.

Back split

Right side: Work across 16 sts, ch 1, turn.

Work even on 16 sc, ch 1, turn for 9 more rows. End off.

Attach yarn in 17th st of jacket back and work left side to correspond to right.

Attach black yarn at left front opening, with right side facing you, and work 1 row of sc around entire edge of jacket, ending at top of right side. Close front of jacket with snaps.

Sleeves

Attach black yarn at underarm opening, pick up 12 sts evenly spaced working in sc.

Work 11 rnds. End off. Make two sleeves.

Rnd 12: Attach white yarn and work 4 rnds even. End off. Fold cuffs back. Make two cuffs.

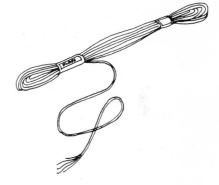

PANTS

With black yarn, ch 24, sl to 1st st to form ring.

Rnd 1: 1 sc in ea st (24 sc).

Rnd 2: 1 sc in ea st of rnd.

Work even until 12 rnds complete.

Right leg

Ch 4, sk 12 sts, attach ch to next st, 1 sc in next 11 sts, 1 sc in ea of ch 4.

Work even on 16 sc until 7 rnds complete.

Rnd 8: ° 1 sc in next st, work dec °. Repeat bet ° four more times. End off.

Left leg

Attach yarn at back of pants and work left leg to correspond to right.

43

COLLAR

With white yarn, ch 16.

Row 1: 1 sc in 2nd ch from hook and in ea ch (15 sc), ch 1, turn.

Row 2: 1 sc in 1st st, 2 sc in next 13 sts, 1 sc in last st (28 sc), ch 1, turn.

Row 3: Sl 9 sts, ch 1, 1 sc in next 9 sts, ch 1, turn.

Row 4: 1 sc in ea st (9 sc), ch 1, turn.

Repeat Row 4 three more times. End off.

Attach yarn in upper left corner and work 1 row of sc to finish edge.

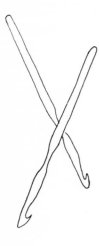

HAT

With black yarn, ch 4, sl to 1st ch to form ring, ch 1.

Rnd 1: 6 sc in center of ring, place marker to indicate beg of rnd, sl to top of ch 1, ch 1.

Rnd 2: 2 sc in ea st (12 sc), sl to top of ch 1, ch 1.

Rnd 3: ° 1 sc in next st, 2 sc in next st °. Repeat bet ° five more times (18 sc), sl to top of ch 1, ch 1.

Rnd 4: ° 1 sc in next 2 sts, 2 sc in next st °. Repeat bet ° five more times (24 sc), sl to top of ch 1, ch 1, place marker to indicate beg of rnd.

Rnd 5: 1 sc in ea st, sl to top of ch 1, ch 1.

Repeat Rnd 5 five more times.

Rnd 11: Ch 3, 1 dc in same st, 2 dc in ea sc of row below (48 dc), sl to top of ch 3, ch 1.

Rnd 12: 1 sc in ea st of rnd below, sl to top of ch 1. End off.

Top rim

Make 1 row of sc in ea st of Rnd 4, working through entire st. End off.

SCARLETT THE SOUTHERN BELLE

COLOR PLATE 1

Make the **basic doll.**

Hair style/Regular with bun using golden brown embroidery floss.
Take 8 strands of embroidery floss about 6 inches long in a color to
match hair and twist tightly together and tie at the ends. Fasten one
end of twist to back of head just above the neck and wind the twist
around in a circle, tucking the other end under. Pin the bun in place
as you go, then tack securely to head with sewing needle and one
strand of thread. Make sure to tack down securely at several points
so bun will not unravel or unwind. (Illustration 29)

ILLUSTRATION 29

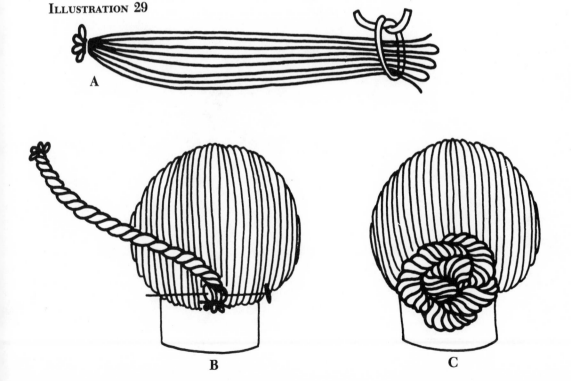

A

B

C

Costume/Dress and Hat

Materials:

   Sock and sweater yarn in yellow and gold
   Steel crochet hook, size #2
   Snaps, size 000
   Yellow mercerized cotton thread
   Embroidery floss in blue, pink, and green.

Gauge:

   6 sts = 1 inch
   7 rows = 1 inch

DRESS

With yellow yarn, ch 24.

Row 1: 2 sc in 2nd ch from hook, 2 sc in ea st across (46 sc), ch 1, turn.

Row 2: 1 sc in ea st across row, ch 1, turn.

Row 3: 1 sc in 1st 5 sts, ch 5, sk 9 sts, 1 sc in next 18 sts, ch 5, sk 9 sts, 1 sc in last 5 sts, ch 1, turn.

Row 4: 1 sc in 1st 5 sts, 1 sc in ea st of ch 5, work dec (insert hook into next st and pull yarn through; pull yarn through next st, then pull yarn through all 3 loops on hook), repeat nine times, 1 sc in ea st of ch 5, 1 sc in last 5 sts, ch 1, turn.

Row 5: 1 sc in ea st across row (28 sts), ch 1, turn.

Repeat Row 5 four more times, ch 3, turn.

Row 9: (Ch 3 counts as 1st dc), 2 dc in same space as ch 3, 3 dc in ea st across row, ch 3, turn.

Row 10: 1 dc in ea st across row, ch 3, turn.

Repeat Row 10 seven more times, ch 3, turn.

Row 18: 1 dc in same space as ch 3, 2 dc in ea st across row, ch 3, turn.

Row 19: 1 dc in ea st across row, ch 1, turn.

Eyelet trim:

Row 20: ° 1 sc in next 3 sts, ch 2, insert hook into 2 loops at base of ch 2 and pull yarn through (eyelet made) °. Repeat bet ° across row, ending with an eyelet. End off.

Sleeves

Attach yarn to underarm opening, ch 3, 1 dc at base of ch 3, 2 dc in next 14 sts evenly spaced around armhole (30 dc), sl to top of ch 3, ch 1. For Row 2, make eyelet trim as in Row 20 of dress. Make two sleeves.

HAT

With gold yarn, ch 4, sl to 1st ch to form ring.

Rnd 1: Ch 3 (ch 3 counts as 1st dc), 11 dc in center of ring, sl to top of ch 3, ch 1.

Rnd 2: 2 sc in ea st (24 sc), ch 1.

Rnd 3: 1 sc in ea st.

Repeat Rnd 3 two more times.

Rnd 6: Ch 3, 2 dc in base of ch 3, 3 dc in next 5 sts, 1 hdc in next 18 sts, sl to top of ch 3.

Rnd 7: 1 hdc in ea dc of row below, sl to 1st hdc of row below, ch 1. Work back sc edging until row complete. End off.

Holding hat, top facing you, attach yarn to Rnd 2 and work 1 row of sc, working through entire st. Sl to 1st st and end off.

With yellow yarn, ch 75. End off. Place around crown of hat and tie in a bow at back of hat. Tack in place.

FLORA THE FLAPPER

COLOR PLATE 1

Make the **basic doll.**

Hair style/Regular with golden brown embroidery floss

Costume/Dress and Hat

Materials:

Sock and sweater yarn in green
Steel crochet hook, size #2
Snaps, size 000
Green mercerized cotton thread

48

Gauge:
   6 sts = 1 inch
   7 rows = 1 inch

FLOUNCE
With green yarn, ch 11.
Row 1: 1 sc in 2nd ch from hook and ea st of ch (10 sc), ch 1, turn.
Row 2: (Working in back loop of row below) 1 sc in ea st, ch 1, turn.
Repeat Row 2 until 50 rows complete. End off. Sew sides together to form skirt.

Dress section
Row 1: Attach yarn at seam. Each row of flounce counts as a st. Pick up 25 sts around as follows: ° pull yarn through 1st st, keep yarn on hook, pull yarn through 2nd st, keep both loops on hook, yo hook and through all 3 loops ° (1 st made). Repeat bet ° (25 sc), ch 1, turn.
Row 2: 1 sc in ea st across row, ch 1, turn.
Repeat Row 2 until 12 rows complete.
Row 13: To make the straps, 1 sc in 1st 5 sts, ch 5, sk 5 sts, 1 sc in next 5 sts, ch 5, sk 5 sts. 1 sc in last 5 sts, ch 1, turn.
Row 14: 1 sc in ea st across including 1 sc in ea ch. End off.
Sew snaps at back opening to close.

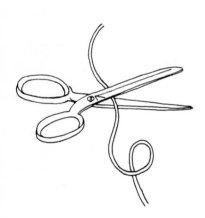

CLOCHE HAT
Ch 4, sl to 1st st of ch to form ring.
Rnd 1: 6 sc in center of ring.
Rnd 2: 2 sc in ea st (12 sc).
Rnd 3: °1 sc in next st, 2 sc in next st °. Repeat bet ° to end of rnd (18 sc).
Rnd 4: °1 sc in next 2 sts, 2 sc in next st °. Repeat bet ° to end of rnd (24 sc).
Rnd 5: ° 1 sc in next 3 sts, 2 sc in next st °. Repeat bet ° to end of rnd (30 sc).
Rnd 6: ° 1 sc in next 4 sts, 2 sc in next st °. Repeat bet ° to end of rnd (36 sc).
Rnd 7: Work even on 36 sc until 12 rnds complete.
Rnd 13: Turn, work back 18 sc, sl 1 st. End off. Fold brim upward in front.

KELLY THE CONTEMPORARY GIRL

COLOR PLATE 2

Make the **basic doll.**

Hair style/Regular with orange or brown embroidery floss or gold with pigtails.
Take 6 strands of embroidery floss about 5 inches long in a color to match hair. With crochet hook, pull the pigtail strands through 3 strands of hair at the side of the head just above the neck. When the strands are centered, tie them together close to the head with red yarn to look like a small bow. Trim the ends to the desired length. Repeat on the other side of the head. (Illustration 30)

ILLUSTRATION 30

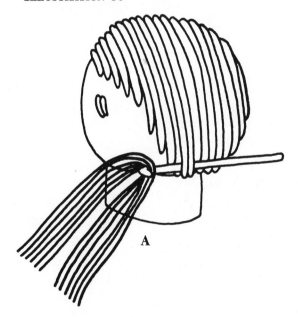

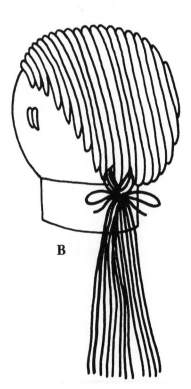

A   B

Costume #1/Jeans and Sweater

Materials:
    Sock and sweater yarn in blue, white, and red
    Steel crochet hook, size #2
    Snaps, size 000
    White mercerized cotton thread
    Small silver beads
    Embroidery floss

Gauge:
    6 sts = 1 inch
    7 rows = 1 inch

SWEATER
With white yarn, ch 17.
Row 1: 1 sc in 2nd ch from hook and ea st of ch (16 sc), ch 1, turn.
Row 2: 2 sc in ea st across (32 sc), ch 1, turn.
Row 3: 1 sc in 1st 5 sts, ch 5, sk 5 sts, 1 sc in next 12 sts, ch 5, sk 5 sts, 1 sc in last 5 sts, ch 1, turn.
Row 4: 1 sc in ea st across, picking up 5 sc in ea ch 5, ch 1, turn.
Row 5: Work even on 32 sc, ch 1, turn, for 9 more rows. End off. Sew silver beads on front of sweater for buttons. Close front with snaps.

Collar
Attach white yarn to right side of sweater neck edge.
Row 1: 1 sc in ea st (16 sc), ch 1, turn.
Row 2: 2 sc in ea st, ch 1, turn.
Row 3: 1 sc in ea st. End off.

Sleeves
Attach white yarn to underarm and work 10 sc evenly spaced. Work even until 12 rnds complete. Make two sleeves.

Trim
With red yarn, sl st in top loop of last row of sleeves. Attach yarn to collar and sl st around edge.

JEANS
With blue yarn, ch 27.
Rnd 1: 1 sc in 2nd st from hook and in ea ch (26 sc).

Rnd 2: 1 sc in ea st to end of rnd.
Rnd 3: Repeat Rnd 2 three more times.

Right leg

Ch 3, sk 13 sts, attach ch to 14th st and work 13 sc, picking up 3 sc in ch 3. Continue to work even on 16 sc until 11 rnds complete.
Rnd 12: Work 2 sc in every other st to inc for bell bottoms.
Rnd 13: 1 sc in ea st, sl 1 st. End off.

Left leg

Attach yarn to center back and work left leg to correspond to right.

Costume #2/Dress, Hat, and Shoes

Materials:
    Sock and sweater yarn in yellow, gold, orange, red orange, and red
    Steel crochet hook, size #2
    Snaps, size 000
    Yellow mercerized cotton thread
Gauge:
    6 sts = 1 inch
    7 rows = 1 inch

DRESS

With yellow yarn, ch 17.
Row 1: 1 sc in 2nd ch from hook, and ea st of ch (16 sc), ch 1, turn.
Row 2: 2 sc in ea st across (32 sc), ch 1, turn.
Row 3: 1 sc in 1st 5 sts, ch 5, sk 5 sts, 1 sc in next 12 sts, ch 5, sk 5 sts, 1 sc in last 5 sts, ch 1, turn.
Row 4: 1 sc in ea st across, picking up 5 sc in ea ch 5, ch 1, turn.
Row 5: Work even on 32 sc, ch 1, turn, for 8 rows, ch 3, turn.
Row 13: 2 dc, ch 1, 2 dc in next st, (shell) ° 1 dc in next 2 sts, 2 dc, ch 1, 2 dc in next st °. Repeat bet ° ending with 1 dc in last st. Join by slipping to top of ch 3. Change to gold yarn, ch 3.
Row 14: ° 2 dc, ch 1, 2 dc in ch 1 space of shell below, 1 dc in next 2 dc below °. Repeat bet ° across row ending 1 dc in last dc, sl to top of ch 3. Change to orange yarn, ch 3.
Row 15: Repeat Row 14, change to red orange yarn.
Row 16: Repeat Row 14, change to red yarn. End off.
Sew on Snaps at back opening to close.

HAT

With yellow yarn, ch 4, sl to 1st ch to form ring.

Rnd 1: 6 sc in center of ring.

Rnd 2: 2 sc in ea st (12 sc).

Rnd 3: ° 1 sc in next st, 2 sc in next st °. Repeat bet ° to end of rnd (18 sc).

Rnd 4: ° 1 sc in next 2 sts, 2 sc in next st °. Repeat bet ° to end of rnd (24 sc).

Rnd 5: Work even on 24 sc for 2 rnds, ch 3.

Rnd 7: 1 dc in base of ch 3, 2 dc in ea st of rnd, sl to top of ch 3, ch 3.

Rnd 8: 1 dc in next 2 sts, 2 dc in next st. ° 1 dc in next 3 sts, 2 dc in next st °. Repeat bet ° to end of rnd, sl to top of ch 3, ch 1.

Rnd 9: Work back sc, working from left to right, 1 sc in ea st, sl to 1st st. End off.

SHOES

Ch 4, sl to 1st ch to form ring.

Rnd 1: 6 sc in center of ring. Place marker to indicate beg of rnd.

Rnd 2: 3 sc in 1st st, 2 sc in next 2 sts, 3 sc in next st, 2 sc in next 2 sts (14 sc).

Rnd 3: Working in top loop of sc in rnd below, 1 sc in ea st.

Rnd 4: 1 sc in ea st, ch 4, sk 7 sts, attach end of ch to 8th st. End off, weave end in, trim.

Make 2.

Costume #3/Coat and Beret

Materials:

    Sock and sweater yarn in camel

    White angora yarn

    Steel crochet hook, size #2

Gauge:

    6 sts = 1 inch

    7 rows = 1 inch

COAT

With camel yarn, ch 11.

Row 1: 1 sc in 2nd ch from hook and ea st of ch (10 sc), ch 1, turn.

Row 2: 2 sc in ea st across (20 sc), ch 1, turn.

Row 3: 2 sc in 1st st, ch 5, sk 5 sts, 1 sc in next 10 sts, ch 5, sk 5 sts,

56

2 sc in last st, ch 1, turn (22 sc).

Row 4: 2 sc in 1st st, 1 sc in ea st across, picking up 5 sc in ea ch 5, 2 sc in last st, ch 1, turn (24 sc).

Row 5: 2 sc in 1st st, 1 sc in ea st across, ch 1, turn.

Row 6: Repeat Row 5 eight more times (32 sc).

Row 14: Work even on 32 sc, ch 1, turn, twelve more times. End off.

Sleeves

Attach yarn at underarm and pick up 12 sc around armhole. Work even for 11 rnds. End off.

Attach white angora yarn and work 4 rnds for cuff. End off. Make two sleeves.

Collar

Row 1: Attach white angora yarn at Row 12 on left side of coat front, work 1 row of sc around to 12 row of right side, turn.

Row 2: Sl 1st st, 1 sc in ea st, sl to last st, turn.

Repeat Row 2 three more times. End off.

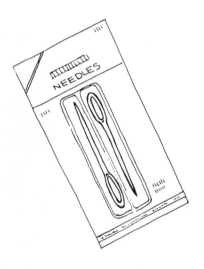

Belt

Ch 3, 1 sc in 2nd ch from hook, 1 sc in last ch, ch 1, turn.

Row 2: 1 sc in next 2 sts, ch 1, turn.

Repeat Row 2 until belt measures 10 inches.

BERET

With white angora yarn, ch 4, sl to 1st ch to form ring.

Rnd 1: 6 sc in center of ring.

Rnd 2: 2 sc in ea st (12 sc).

Rnd 3: ° 1 sc in next st, 2 sc in next st °. Repeat bet ° to end of rnd (18 sc).

Rnd 4: ° 1 sc in next 2 sts, 2 sc in next st °. Repeat bet ° to end of rnd (24 sc).

Rnd 5: Work even on 24 sc for 2 rnds.

Rnd 7: Work dec, pull up loop in next 2 sts, yo hook and through all 3 loops, continue dec to end of rnd. End off.

5
Dolls From Many Lands

Dolls from Many Lands contains instructions for five different dolls
in their native costumes. Although each doll can stand alone, the
entire group would make a charming collection.

   Of all the dolls in the book, I admit that these were the most
fun for me. Although the sizes and shapes of all the dolls are the
same, I had a warm feeling of many peoples coming together as an
international family or worldwide group as I worked on these dolls.

Chinook the Eskimo is snugly wrapped in a fur outfit trimmed in white angora. The warm boots are fur-trimmed as well.

Little Fox the American Indian doll has a two-piece suit with fringes on the sleeves and pants, and a bead necklace. The long braids are a typical Indian hair style.

Mary Lou the Jamaican is made with brown yarn. She

wears a jaunty red two-piece outfit complete with a basket of fruit she carries on her head.

Myoshi the Japanese girl is made with yellow yarn. She is clothed in a blue-flowered kimono tied with a white obi. Her hair style gives her a geisha look.

Juanita the Spanish doll wears a beautiful flamenco dress, a lacy black shawl, and a flower behind her ear.

CHINOOK
THE ESKIMO

COLOR PLATE 3

Make the **basic doll.**

Hair style/Regular with black embroidery floss

Costume/Jacket, Pants, and Boots

Materials:
  Sock and sweater yarn in brown and yellow
  White angora or mohair yarn
  Steel crochet hook, size #2
  Snaps, size 000
  White mercerized cotton thread
Gauge:
  6 sts = 1 inch
  7 rows = 1 inch

JACKET
With brown yarn, ch 17.
Row 1: 1 sc in 2nd ch from hook, ch 1, turn (16 sc).
Row 2: 2 sc in ea st across (32 sc), ch 1, turn.
Row 3: 1 sc in 1st 5 sts, ch 5, sk 5 sts, 1 sc in next 12 sts, ch 5, sk 5 sts, 1 sc in last 5 sts, ch 1, turn.
Row 4: 1 sc in ea st across, picking up 5 sc in ea ch 5, ch 1, turn.
Row 5: 1 sc in ea st across, ch 1, turn.
Work even on 32 sc, ch 1, turn for 15 more rows. End off.

Sleeves
Pick up 13 sc evenly spaced around armhole. Work even for 12 rnds.
Make two sleeves.

63

Hood

Attach yarn to right side of neck.
Row 1: Pick up 16 sc, ch 1, turn.
Row 2: Work even on 16 sc, ch 1, turn, until 14 rows complete.
Fold hood in half and sl tog to close top. End off.

Fur trim

With white angora or mohair yarn, attach to center back and work 1 row of sc around entire jacket including hood, sl to 1st st.
Row 2: Working from left to right, work 1 row of back sc in ea st, sl to 1st st. End off.
Repeat fur trim around sleeves.
Close jacket front with snaps.

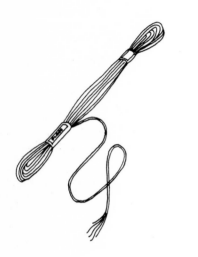

PANTS

With brown yarn, ch 24, sl to 1st ch to form ring.
Rnd 1: 1 sc in ea ch (24 sc).
Rnd 2: Work even on 24 sc until 6 rnds complete.

Right leg

Ch 4, sk 12 sts, attach ch to 13th st.
Work around to ch, pick up 4 sc in ch 4.
Work even on 16 sc until 11 rnds complete. End off.

Left leg

Attach yarn at center back and work left leg to correspond with right.

BOOTS

With yellow yarn, ch 12, sl st to 1st ch to form ring.
Rnd 1: 1 sc in ea ch (12 sc).
Rnd 2: Work even on 12 sc until 6 rnds complete.
Row 7: Work 6 sc, ch 1, turn.
Row 8: 1 sc in 2nd st, 1 sc in next 4 sts, ch 1, turn.
Row 9: 1 sc in 2nd st, 1 sc in next 3 sts. End off. Make two boots.
Add fur trim as for jacket to the top edge of boot.

Soles

Ch 4, sl to 1st ch to form ring.
Rnd 1: 6 sc in center of ring.

Rnd 2: 3 sc in 1st st, 2 sc in next 2 sts, 3 sc in next st, 2 sc in next 2 sts, sl to next st.

Rnd 3: 1 sc in next st, 3 sc in next st, 1 sc in next 5 sts, 3 sc in next st, 1 sc in next 5 sts, sl to next st. Make two soles.

Sl st the sole to the bottom of boot. End off.

LITTLE FOX THE AMERICAN INDIAN

COLOR PLATE 1

Make the **basic doll.**

Hair style/Regular with braids using black embroidery floss.
Take 6 strands of black yarn about 8 inches long. With crochet hook, pull them through 3 strands of hair at the side of the head just above the neck. Take 3 groups of 4 strands each and braid them. When braid is about 2 inches long, tie tightly with a single strand of black yarn and trim ends. Repeat on the other side of the head. (Illustration 31)

ILLUSTRATION 31

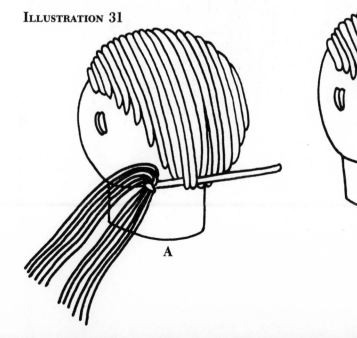

A

B

Costume/Shirt and Pants

Materials:
    Sock and sweater yarn in camel and black
    Steel crochet hook, size #2
    Small beads and a beading needle
    Snaps, size 000
    Camel mercerized cotton thread

Gauge:
    6 sts = 1 inch
    7 rows = 1 inch

SHIRT

With camel yarn, ch 17.
Row 1: 1 sc in 2nd ch from hook and ea ch (16 sc), ch 1, turn.
Row 2: 2 sc in ea st (32 sc), ch 1, turn.
Row 3: 1 sc in 1st 5 sts, sk 5 sts, 1 sc in next 12 sts, ch 5, sk 5 sts, 1 sc in last 5 sts, ch 1, turn.
Row 4: 1 sc in ea st, picking up 5 sc in ea ch 5 (32 sc), ch 1, turn.
Work even on 32 sc until 20 rows complete. End off.
Fasten back of shirt with snaps.
String beads on thread for necklace.

Sleeves

Attach yarn at underarm and pick up 12 sc evenly spaced around armhole.
Work even on 12 sc until 12 rnds complete. End off.
Make an even row of fringe starting at center inside of underarm to edge of sleeve. Trim to ½ inch. Make two sleeves.

PANTS

With camel yarn, ch 24, sl to 1st ch to form ring.
Rnd 1: 1 sc in ea st of ch (24 sc).
Work even until 6 rnds complete, ch 4.

Right leg

Sk 12 sts, attach ch to next st, work 1 sc in next 12 sts, pick up 4 sc in ch 4.
Work even on 16 sc until 14 rnds complete. End off.

Left leg

Attach yarn at center back and work left leg to correspond to right. Make an even row of fringe down side of leg from top of pants to 2 rnds from bottom. Trim to ½ inch.

NECKLACE

String color beads on thread. Knot ends. Trim.

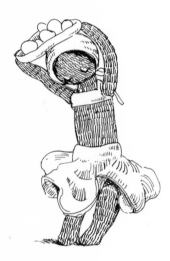

MARY LOU THE JAMAICAN

COLOR PLATE 3

Make the **basic doll** except use brown yarn and sew eyes in beige embroidery floss.

Hair style/Regular with black embroidery floss

Costume/Bra, Skirt, Kerchief, and Bowl

Materials:

> Sock and sweater yarn in scarlet and yellow
> Steel crochet hook, size #2
> Snaps, size 000
> Scarlet mercerized cotton thread
> Miniature plastic fruit
> White household glue

Gauge:

> 6 sts = 1 inch
> 7 rows = 1 inch

68

BRA

With scarlet yarn, ch 50. End off.

Row 1: Attach yarn in 20th st of ch, work 10 sc, ch 1, turn.

Row 2: Sk 1st st, work 8 sc, ch 1, turn.

Row 3: Sk 1st st, work 6 sc, ch 25 for neck tie. End off.

Attach yarn to upper right corner of bra and ch 25. End off.

SKIRT

With scarlet yarn, ch 27.

Row 1: 1 sc in 2nd ch from hook and ea st of ch, ch 1, turn (26 sc).

Row 2: 1 sc in 2nd st and ea st across row, ch 1, turn.

Row 3: 1 sc in ea st across, ch 5, turn.

Row 4: 1 tr in 1st st, ° 5 tr, ch 1 in next st, 1 tr, ch 1 in next 5 sts °. Repeat bet ° three more times, ch 5, turn.

Row 5: (Ch 5 counts as 1st tr) Work in tr of row below, 1 tr, ch 1 in next 6 sts, ° 5 tr, ch 1 in next st, 1 tr, ch 1 in next 9 sts °. Repeat bet ° three more times, ending 1 tr, ch 1 in last 7 sts, ch 5, turn.

Row 6: 1 tr, ch 1 in 2nd st and next 3 sts, ° 5 tr, ch 1 in next st, 1 tr, ch 1 in next 13 sts °. Repeat bet ° three more times, ending 1 tr, ch 1 in last 9 sts, ch 3, turn.

Row 7: 1 sc in ea st across. End off.

Sew up back to just below waist and fasten with a snap.

KERCHIEF

Row 1: With scarlet yarn, ch 3, 1 sc in last st of ch, ch 1, turn.

Row 2: 2 sc in 1st st, 1 sc in next 2 sts, 2 sc in last st, ch 1, turn.

Row 3: 2 sc in 1st st, 1 sc in next 2 sts, 2 sc in last st, ch 1, turn.

Continue to work 2 sc in 1st st, 2 sc in last st, 1 sc in ea st in bet, ch 1, turn, until 12 rows complete, ch 15 for tie. End off.

Attach yarn to opposite side and ch 15. End off.

Tie kerchief around head at back.

BOWL

With yellow yarn, ch 3, sl to 1st st to form ring.

Rnd 1: 6 sc in center of ring.

Rnd 2: 2 sc in ea st (12 sc).

Rnd 3: ° 1 sc in next st, 2 sc in next st °. Repeat bet ° to end of rnd (18 sc).

Rnd 4: ° 1 sc in next 2 sts, 2 sc in next st °. Repeat bet ° to end of rnd (24 sc).

70

Rnd 5: ° 1 sc in next 3 sts, 2 sc in next st °. Repeat bet ° to end of rnd (30 sc).

Rnd 6: ° 1 sc in next 4 sts, 2 sc in next st °. Repeat bet ° to end of rnd (36 sc).

Rnd 7: ° 1 sc in next 5 sts, 2 sc in next st °. Repeat bet ° to end of rnd (42 sc).

Rnd 8: ° 1 sc in next 6 sts, 2 sc in next st °. Repeat bet ° to end of rnd (48 sc).

Rnd 9: ° 1 sc in next 7 sts, 2 sc in next st °. Repeat bet ° to end of rnd (54 sc).

Rnds 10 and 11 work even, 1 sc in ea st. End off.

Securely attach bowl to center of head on top of kerchief. Pour small amount of white household glue in center of bowl to hold in place 5 or 6 pieces of small plastic fruit.

MYOSHI THE JAPANESE GIRL

COLOR PLATE 3

Make the **basic doll** except use pale yellow yarn and make the soles of the feet with black yarn. Sew or slip stitch the soles to the feet with black yarn to resemble sandals.

Hair style/Regular with elaborate braids using black embroidery floss.

Take 24 strands of black yarn about 12 inches long and fasten tightly at one end with a double strand of black yarn. Divide into 3 sections of 8 strands each and make a braid about 8 inches long. Tie securely with double strand of black yarn and trim close to tie. Fold end under and pin to top center of head with braid going down the back. Pin braid at neck and wind around head twice, tucking the end under the top knot. When pinned in place, tack securely to head with black cotton thread. (Illustration 32)

ILLUSTRATION 32

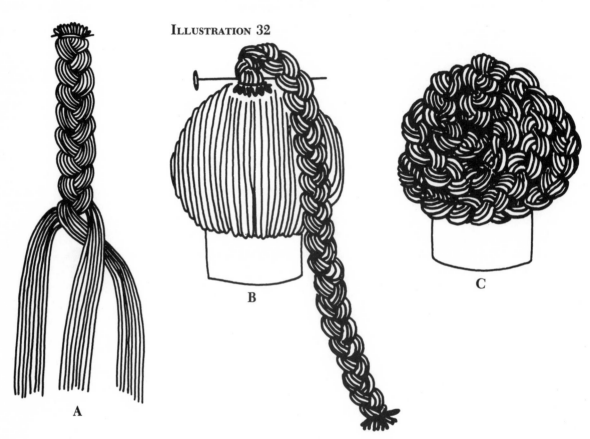

A

B

C

Costume/Kimono and Obi

Materials:

Sock and sweater yarn in blue, white, and black
Steel crochet hook, size #2
Embroidery floss in assorted colors and black
Embroidery needle
Snaps, size 000
Black and white mercerized cotton thread.

72

Gauge:
> 6 sts = 1 inch
> 7 rows = 1 inch

KIMONO

With blue yarn, ch 21.

Row 1: 1 sc in 2nd ch from hook and ea st of ch (20 sc), ch 1, turn.

Row 2: 1 sc in ea st across, ch 1, turn.

Row 3: 1 sc in 1st st, 2 sc in ea st across row, 1 sc in last st (38 sc), ch 1, turn.

Row 4: 1 sc in 1st 6 sts, ch 6, sk 6 sts, 1 sc in next 14 sts, ch 6, sk 6 sts, 1 sc in last 6 sts, ch 1, turn.

Row 5: 1 sc in ea st across row, picking up 6 sc in ea ch 6, ch 1, turn.

Row 6: 1 sc in ea st across row, ch 1, turn.

Repeat Row 6 twenty-seven more times. End off.

Sleeves

Pick up 15 sc around armhole.

Work even for 11 rnds. End off. Make two sleeves.

Finishing edge

Start at center back and work 1 row of sc around entire garment for finishing edge.

Floral trim

Using brightly colored embroidery floss, make flowers and leaves at random. Use the daisy and French knot stitches (see Embroidery Stitch Glossary, page 172).

OBI

With white yarn, ch 28.

Row 1: 1 sc in 2nd ch from hook and ea st of ch (27 sc), ch 1, turn.

Row 2: 1 sc in ea st across.

Repeat Row 2 two more times. End off.

Part two

Ch 6, 1 sc in 2nd ch from hook and ea st of ch (5 sc), ch 1, turn. Repeat Row 2 until 18 rows complete, ch 1, work 1 row of sc around entire edge to finish off, sl to 1st st. End off.

Fold the top over and secure.

Attach to right side of belt and fasten with snap.

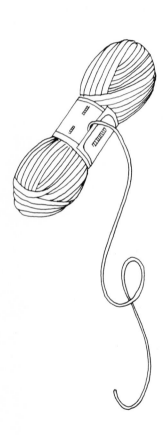

JUANITA THE SPANISH GIRL

COLOR PLATE 3

Make the **basic doll.**

Hair style/Regular with a bun using black embroidery floss. Take 6 strands of embroidery floss or yarn about 6 inches long in a color to match the hair. Tie each end with a single strand and trim ends. Secure one end at back of head just above neck. Twist and wind around to form a bun. Pin to head and stitch securely with black cotton thread. (Illustration 33)

ILLUSTRATION 33

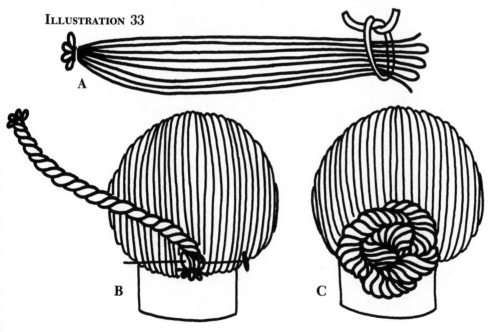

Costume/Dress, Shawl, and Flower

Materials:

    Sock and sweater yarn in red, gold, and black
    Steel crochet hook, size #2
    Snaps, size 000
    Black and red mercerized cotton thread

75

Gauge:

    6 sts = 1 inch

    7 rows = 1 inch

DRESS

With red yarn, ch 28 for top of dress.

Row 1: 1 sc in 2nd ch from hook, 1 sc in ea ch (27 sc), ch 1, turn.

Row 2: 1 sc in ea st across row, ch 1, turn.

Row 3: Repeat Row 2 until 8 rows complete.

Row 9: ° 1 sc in 1st st, 2 sc in next st °. Repeat bet ° to end of row, ch 3, turn.

Row 10: (Ch 3 counts as 1st dc), 1 dc in ea st across row (37 dc), ch 1, turn.

Row 11: 1 sc in ea st across row, ch 3, turn.

Repeat Rows 10 and 11 four more times, ch 4, turn.

Row 20: (Ch 4 counts as 1st tr), 3 tr in base of ch 4, ° 4 tr in next st°. Repeat bet ° to end of row. End off.

Row 21: Attach gold yarn to bottom of hemline ruffle. 1 sc in 1st 3 sts, ch 2. 1 sc in same st as last sc, ° 1 sc in next 3 sts, ch 2, 1 sc in same st as last sc °. Repeat bet ° to end of row. End off.

Right front

With red yarn, attach on right side at top of dress in 9th st from end, sl 1 st, 1 sc in next 4 sts, ch 1, turn.

Row 2: Sk 1st st, 1 sc in next 3 sts, ch 1, turn.

Row 3: Sk 1st st, 1 sc in next 2 sts, ch 1, turn.

Row 4: Sk 1st st, 1 sc in next st, ch 6, attach end of ch to 4th st on top of right side of dress. End off.

Left front

Attach yarn 1 st over from right front and work left side to correspond to right.

Additional ruffle made separately.

Ruffle

With red yarn, ch 51.

Row 1: 1 sc in 2nd st and ea st across (50 dc), ch 4, turn.

Row 2: 3 tr in base of ch 4, 4 tr in ea st across. End off.

Row 3: Attach gold yarn and repeat Row 21 of dress.

Pin separate ruffle just above hemline ruffle and attach. Sew up back of dress to just below waist and close top of dress with snaps.

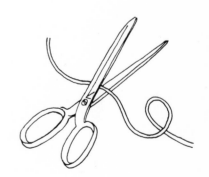

FLOWER

With red yarn, ch 4, sl to 1st ch to form ring.

Rnd 1: ° ch 3, 1 dc in center of ring, sl st in center of ring (petal made) °. Repeat bet ° three more times. Tie ends together and weave in.

Tack flower at side of head.

SHAWL

With black yarn,

Row 1: Ch 4. In 1st st of ch, work 1 dc, (ch 2, point)(1 dc, ch 1, 1 dc shell), ch 4, turn.

Row 2: at base of ch 4, work 1 dc, ch 1, in ch 2 space of row below, work (1 dc, ch 1, 1 dc shell) ch 2, (shell), ch 1, in 3rd st of ch at end of row, work 1 dc, ch 1, 1 sc, ch 4, turn.

Row 3: at base of ch 4, work 1 dc, ch 1, work (shell) in next ch 1 space between shells of row below, ch 1, in ch 2 space at point, work 1 shell, ch 2, 1 shell, ch 1, work 1 shell in ch 1 space between next two shells of row below, ch 1, work 1 shell in 3rd st of ch at end of row below, ch 4, turn.

Repeat Row 3 five more times, increasing 1 shell on either side of point each row, ending with 16 shells, ch 5, turn.

Row 9: 1 sc in ch 1 space bet shells of row below. ° Ch 5, 1 sc in next ch 1 space bet shells of row below °. Repeat bet ° all around shawl, ending with ch 5, sl to 3rd st of ch at the end of row, turn.

Row 10: Sl 3 sts of ch 5 below,° ch 5, 1 sc in center of ch 5 of row below °. Repeat bet °, ending with 1 sc in center of last ch 5 of row below. End off. Weave end of yarn through several sts of shawl to secure.

6
Storybook Characters

The Storybook Characters are for fantasy and fun. They lead the way
back to the adventure, romance, and suspense in all the stories
you read as a child, and in the stories you in turn read to your children.
I hope these dolls will transport you to a fanciful and beautiful place
while you are making them and delight those who receive them.

The diminutive girl with a flower umbrella can become any number of well-known storybook characters. You might add a red cape to her costume or three bear companions to change her role.

Richie, the little baseball player, and his pet Champ are characters in any traditional story of a boy and his dog. Why

not make a whole team for a child with a big imagination?

In every fairy tale there is always a princess—in a tower, at a ball, or under a spell. The princess doll you make will capture the heart of all who see her in her gold and white gown, gold crown, and furry white cape.

STORYBOOK GIRL

COLOR PLATE 4

Make the **basic doll.**

Hair style/Regular with yellow embroidery thread.

Costume/Dress, Apron, Panties, and Cap

Materials:
    Sock and sweater yarn in blue and white
    Steel crochet hook, size #2
    Embroidery floss in pink and green
    Snaps, size 000
    Blue mercerized cotton thread

Gauge:
    6 sts = 1 inch
    7 rows = 1 inch

DRESS
With blue yarn, ch 17.
Row 1: 1 sc in 2nd ch from hook and in ea st across (16 sc), ch 1, turn.
Row 2: 2 sc in ea st across row (32 sc), ch 1, turn.
Row 3: 1 sc in 1st 5 sts, ch 5, sk 5 sts, 1 sc in next 12 sts, ch 5, sk 5 sts, 1 sc in last 5 sts, ch 1, turn.
Row 4: 1 sc in ea st across, picking up 5 sc in ea ch 5, ch 1, turn.
Row 5: Work even on 32 sc until 10 rows complete, ch 3, turn.
Row 11: 2 dc in ea st across (64 dc), ch 1, turn.
Row 12: 1 sc in 1st st, ° ch 1, sk 1st st, 1 sc in next st °. Repeat bet ° to end of row, ch 3, turn.
Row 13: ° 1 sc in sc, 1 dc in ch 1 space °. Repeat bet ° to end of row. Repeat Rows 12 and 13 three more times. End off.
Sew dress from bottom to below waist and close top with snaps.

Sleeves

Attach yarn at underarm, ch 3, work 2 dc 10 times, sl to top of ch 3.
Rnd 2: Dec as follows: ° insert hook in 1st st, pull loop through, insert hook in 2nd st, pull loop through, yo hook and through all 3 loops °. Repeat bet ° to end of rnd. Sl to top of next st. End off. Make two sleeves.

APRON

With white yarn, ch 10.
Row 1: 1 dc in 4th ch from hook, 2 dc in ea ch (14 dc), ch 1, turn.
Row 2: 1 sc in ea st across row, ch 3, turn.
Row 3: 1 dc in ea st across, ch 1, turn.
Repeat Rows 2 and 3 three more times. End off.

Bib

Attach yarn in upper right corner and ch 3, 1 sc in 2nd st and ea st across (7 dc), ch 1, turn.
Row 2: 1 sc in ea st across, ch 3, turn.
Row 3: 1 dc in ea st across, ch 1, do not end off but work down side of bib. Work 1 row of sc around entire apron to finish but do not end off.

Ruffle

Ch 3, ° sl to next sc, ch 3, sl in same sc °. Repeat bet ° around entire apron. End off.

Ties

Attach yarn to waist at right side and ch 25. End off. Repeat for left side.

PANTIES

With white yarn, ch 25, sl to 1st ch to form ring.
Rnd 1: 1 sc in ea st (25 sc).
Rnd 2: Insert hook in top loop only, 1 sc in ea st to end of rnd.
Repeat Rnd 2 two more times.

Right leg

Ch 3, sk 12 sts, work 1 rnd of sc, picking up 3 sc in ch 3.
Rnd 2: ° Ch 3, sl to next st °. Repeat bet ° to end of rnd. End off.

Left leg

Attach yarn to center back and work left leg to correspond to right.

CAP

With white yarn, ch 4, sl to 1st ch to form ring.

Rnd 1: 6 sc in center of ring. Place marker to indicate beg of rnd.

Rnd 2: 2 sc in ea st (12 sc).

Rnd 3: ° 1 sc in next st, 2 sc in next st °. Repeat bet ° to end of rnd.

Rnd 4: ° 1 sc in next 2 sts, 2 sc in next st °. Repeat bet ° to end of rnd.

Rnd 5: ° 1 sc in next 3 sts, 2 sc in next st °. Repeat bet ° to end of rnd.

Rnd 6: ° 1 sc in next 4 sts, 2 sc in next st °. Repeat bet ° to end of rnd.

Rnds 7 and 8: Work even on 36 sc.

Rnd 9: 1 sc in ea st of rnd.

Rnd 10: Dec ea st by pulling up a loop in next 2 sts, yo hook and through all 3 loops. Continue to end of rnd.

Rnd 11: Ch 3, sl to base of ch 3, sl to next st °, ch 3, sl in same st, sl to next st °. Repeat bet ° to end of rnd.

Embroider small flowers and leaves on cap and apron using French knots and daisy stitch.

FLOWER UMBRELLA

COLOR PLATE 4 AND 9

Materials:

Sock and sweater yarn in pink, gold, and green

Steel crochet hook, size #2

Stem wire

Gauge:

6 sts = 1 inch

7 rows = 1 inch

CENTER
With gold yarn, ch 4, sl to 1st ch to form ring.
Rnd 1: 8 sc in center of ring.
Rnd 2: Ch 3, 3 dc in 1st st, remove hook from last dc, insert hook into top of ch 3, and back into last dc, yo hook and pull loop through tightly (petal formed), ch 2, ° 4 dc in next st, remove hook, insert hook into 1st dc and 4th dc, yo hook and pull loop through tightly, ch 2 °. Repeat bet ° six more times, sl to top of ch 3. End off.

PETALS
° Attach pink yarn in any ch 2 space of center, ch 3.
Row 1: 5 dc in ch 2 space, ch 3, turn.
Row 2: 1 sc in ea st, ch 3, turn.
Row 3: Sk 1st st, 1 sc in next 4 sts, ch 1, turn.
Row 4: 1 sc in ea st, ch 1, turn.
Row 5: Sk 1st st, 1 sc in next 2 sts. End off. °
Repeat bet ° in ea ch 2 space of center for 8 petals.
Attach pink yarn to lower right side of any petal, ° work 1 row of sc around edge of petal. When you reach the top center st, work 3 sc, then continue down left side of petal. Sl into ch 2 space of petal, sl to next petal and continue from ° until ea petal is complete.

STEM
With green yarn, ch 4.
Rnd 1: Working through top loop of ch, 1 sc in ea st (4 sc).
Continue working 1 sc in top loop of sc below. This will form a tube. Work in rnds until stem measures 5 inches but do not end off.
Ch 15, ° 1 sc in 2nd ch from hook, 1 hdc in next 2 ch, 1 dc in next 2 ch, 1 tr in next 2 ch, 1 dc in next 2 ch, 1 hdc in next 2 ch, 1 sc in next 2 ch, ° sl to top of stem. Ch 15, repeat bet °. End off.
Slip a stem wire up through stem tube and attach to flower between petals. You may want to press the petals flat.

BaBY BeaR

Materials:

    Sock and sweater yarn in brown and pink

    Steel crochet hook, size #2

    Embroidery floss in black, white, and pink

    Embroidery needle

    Brown mercerized cotton thread

Gauge:

    6 sts = 1 inch

    7 rows = 1 inch

HEAD

With brown yarn, ch 4, sl to 1st ch to form ring.

Rnd 1: 6 sc in center of ring.

Rnd 2: 2 sc in ea st (12 sc).

Rnd 3: * 1 sc in next st, 2 sc in next st *. Repeat bet * to end of rnd (18 sc).

Rnd 4: * 1 sc in next 2 sts, 2 sc in next st *. Repeat bet * to end of rnd (24 sc).

Rnd 5: Work even on 24 sc until 9 rnds complete.

Rnd 10: * 1 sc in next 2 sts [insert hook into next st and pull yarn through, insert hook into next st, yo hook and through all 3 loops (dec made)] *. Repeat bet * to end of rnd.

Rnd 11: * 1 sc in next st, (dec) next 2 sts *. Repeat bet * to end of rnd.

Stuffing

Insert fiberfill through opening and stuff firmly, making head as round as possible. Finish head by working dec until opening is completely closed. End off by cutting yarn and pulling through last st. Weave end through and trim.

Sew eyes with white and black embroidery floss; sew nose with pink.

Ears

With pink yarn, ch 3, sl to 1st ch to form ring.
Rnd 1: 6 sc in center of ring. End off.
Rnd 2: Attach brown yarn and work 2 sc in ea st (12 sc), sl to next st.
End off. Make two ears.

Snout

With brown yarn, ch 3, sl to 1st st to form ring.
Rnd 1: 3 sc in 1st st, 2 sc in next 2 sts, 3 sc in next st, 2 sc in next 2 sts.
Rnd 2: 1 sc in ea st. End off.
Sew snout and ears to head.

BODY

Work the same as head for 1st 4 rnds.
Work even on 24 sc until 15 rnds complete.
Rnd 16: Same as Rnd 10 for head.
Rnd 17: Same as Rnd 11 for head.

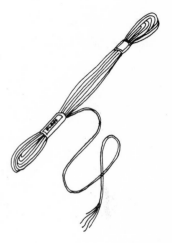

Stuffing

Insert fiberfill through opening and stuff firmly, molding into a body shape. Finish body by working dec until opening is completely closed. End off by cutting yarn and pulling through last st. Weave end through and trim.

ARMS AND LEGS

With pink yarn, ch 4, sl to 1st st to form ring.
Rnd 1: 8 sc in center of ring, sl to 1st st. End off.
Rnd 2: Attach brown yarn, working through back loop only, 1 sc in ea st.
Rnd 3: Work even on 8 sc until 4 rnds complete. End off. Make two arms and two legs.

Stuffing

Insert fiberfill through opening and stuff firmly into arms and legs. Finish arms and legs by working dec until openings are completely closed. End off by cutting yarn and pulling through last st. Weave end through and trim.
Sew arms directly at sides 2 rnds below head.
Sew legs to bottom of body in line with arms.

RED CAPE WITH HOOD

COLOR PLATE 4

Make the **basic doll.**

Hair style/Regular with brown embroidery thread.

Costume/Dress and shoes (instructions on page 56) and Red Cape with Hood

Materials:
    Sock and sweater yarn in red
    Steel crochet Hook, size #2
Gauge:
    6 sts = 1 inch
    7 rows = 1 inch

CAPE

With red yarn, ch 17.

Row 1: 1 sc in 2nd ch from hook, 1 sc in ea st of ch (16 sc), ch 3, turn.

Row 2: (Ch 3 counts as 1st dc), 1 dc in 1st st, 2 dc in ea st across (32 dc), ch 1, turn.

Row 3: 1 sc in ea dc, ch 3, turn.

Row 4: 1 dc in same st as ch 3, ° 1 dc in next st, 2 dc in next st °. Repeat bet ° to end of row, ch 1, turn.

Row 5: 1 sc in ea st across, ch 3, turn.

Row 6: 1 sc in 1st st, ° 2 dc in next st, 1 dc in next st °. Repeat bet ° to end of row, ch 1, turn.

Row 7: 1 sc in ea st, ch 3, turn.

Row 8: 1 sc in ea st. End off.

Hood

Attach yarn to top of right side of cape, work 1 sc in ea st (16 sc), ch 3, turn.

Row 2: Work 1 dc in ea st, ch 1, turn.

Row 3: 1 sc in ea st, ch 3, turn.

Repeat Rows 2 and 3 four more times.

Fold hood together and sl st top. End off.

Attach yarn at center back of cape and work 1 row of sc for finishing edge.

Ties

Attach yarn at neck edge and ch 20. End off. Repeat on other side.

RICHIE THE BASEBALL PLAYER

COLOR PLATE 5

Make the **basic doll** except crochet the legs with white yarn. Follow the basic pattern up to Rnd 14. End off. Attach black yarn and work 1 row even.

Row 16: Work 5 sc, ch 1, turn.

Row 17: 1 sc in 2nd st, 1 sc in next 3 sts, ch 1, turn.

Row 18: 1 sc in 2nd st, 1 sc in next 2 sts. End off. Make sole in black; attach to foot with black yarn.

Hair style/Regular with brown embroidery floss.

Costume/Shirt, Pants, Hat, and Glove

Materials:

    Sock and sweater yarn in red, white, black, and brown

    Steel crochet hook, size #2

    Snaps, size 000

    White and brown mercerized cotton thread

    Tapestry needle, #18

92

Gauge:

    6 sts = 1 inch

    7 rows = 1 inch

SHIRT

With red yarn, ch 17.

Row 1: 1 sc in 2nd ch from hook and in ea ch (16 sc), ch 1, turn.

Row 2: 2 sc in ea st (32 sc), ch 1, turn.

Row 3: 1 sc in 1st 5 sts, ch 5, sk 5 sts, 1 sc in next 12 sts, ch 5, sk 5 sts, 1 sc in last 5 sts, ch 1, turn.

Row 4: 1 sc in ea st, picking up 5 sc in ea ch 5, ch 1, turn.

Row 5: 1 sc in ea st across, ch 1, turn.

Repeat Row 5, working even on 32 sc, ch 1, turn, nine more times. End off.

Sleeves

Attach yarn at underarm. Pick up 11 sc evenly spaced around armhole. Work even until 5 rnds complete. End off. Make two sleeves.

Trim

With white yarn, attach to neck and work 1 row of sc (16 sc). Work 1 row of sc around sleeves.

Close shirt front with snaps.

PANTS

With white yarn, ch 24, sl to 1st ch to form ring.

Rnd 1: 1 sc in ea st (24 sc).

Work even until 6 rnds complete, ch 4.

Right leg

Sk 12 sts, attach ch to next st. Work 12 sc, pick up 4 sc in ch 4. Work even on 16 sc until 11 rnds complete.

Rnd 12: Work dec, 1 sc in next 8 sts, dec, sl to next st. End off.

Left leg

Attach yarn at center back and work left leg to correspond with right.

Stripe

With #18 tapestry needle, sew ch st in red yarn directly down sides of pants.

94

HAT

With white yarn, ch 4, sl to 1st st to form ring.
Rnd 1: 6 sc in center of ring.
Rnd 2: 2 sc in ea st (12 sc).
Rnd 3: * 1 sc in next st, 2 sc in next st *. Repeat bet * to end of rnd.
Rnd 4: * 1 sc in next 2 sts, 2 sc in next st *. Repeat bet * to end of rnd.
Rnd 5: Work even on 24 sc for 3 rnds. End off.

Bill

Attach red yarn to last st of Rnd 7, work 9 sc, turn.
Row 2: 2 sc in 2nd st, and next 4 sts, sl to next st, turn.
Row 3: 1 sc in 2nd st, and next 11 sts, sl to last st. End off.

GLOVE

With brown yarn, ch 7.
Row 1: 1 sc in 2nd ch from hook and ea st of ch (6 sc), ch 3, turn.
Row 2: 2 dc in base of ch 3, sl to next st, 1 sc in next 3 sts, 2 sc in last st, ch 1, turn.
Row 3: 1 sc in next 4 sts, 2 sc in last st, ch 1, turn.
Row 4: 1 sc in next 5 sts, 2 sc in last st, ch 1, turn.
Row 5: 1 sc in next 6 sts, 2 sc in last st, ch 1, turn.
Row 6: 1 sc in 2nd st, 1 sc in next 6 sts, ch 1, turn.
Row 7: 1 sc in 2nd st, 1 sc in next 5 sts, ch 1, turn.
Row 8: 1 sc in 2nd st, 1 sc in next 4 sts, sl to edge. End off. Make two pieces.
Hold two pieces tog; attach yarn under thumb and sl st tog around thumb and around glove to left side at the bottom. Put the glove on the right hand of the doll and tack in place.

THE LITTLE DOG CHAMP

COLOR PLATE 5

Materials:

    Sock and sweater yarn in camel and black
    Steel crochet hook, size #2
    Embroidery floss in blue and black
    Embroidery needle
    Black and camel mercerized cotton thread

COLOR PLATE 1

FRONT ROW: Little Fox (page 65); Priscilla (page 39); John (page 41)
BACK ROW: Scarlett (page 45); Flora (page 48)

COLOR PLATE 2
Kelly in Coat and Beret (page 56); in Dress, Hat, and Shoes (page 54); and in
Jeans and Sweater (page 53)

COLOR PLATE 3
Myoshi (page 71); Mary Lou (page 68); Chinook (page 63); and Juanita (page 75)

COLOR PLATE 4
Baby Bear (page 87); Storybook Girl with Flower Umbrella (pages 83 and 85);
Fairytale Princess (page 103); and Storybook Girl in Red Cape with Hood
(page 91)

Gauge:
    6 sts = 1 inch
    7 rows = 1 inch

HEAD

With camel yarn, ch 4, sl to 1st ch to form ring.

Rnd 1: 6 sc in center of ring. Place marker to indicate beg of rnd.

Rnd 2: 2 sc in ea st (12 sc).

Rnd 3: ° 1 sc in next st, 2 sc in next st °. Repeat bet ° to end of rnd (18 sc).

Rnd 4: ° 1 sc in next 2 sts, 2 sc in next st °. Repeat bet ° to end of rnd (24 sc).

Rnd 5: Work even on 24 sc until 9 rnds complete.

Rnd 10: ° 1 sc in next 2 sts [insert hook into next st and pull yarn through; keeping yarn on hook, insert hook into next st, yo hook and through all 3 loops (dec made)] °. Repeat bet ° to end of rnd.

Rnd 11: ° 1 sc in next st, (dec) next 2 sts °. Repeat bet ° to end of rnd.

Stuffing

Insert fiberfill through opening and stuff firmly, making head as round as possible. Finish head by working dec until opening is completely closed. End off by cutting yarn and pulling through last st. Weave end through and trim.

Snout

With black yarn, ch 3, sl to 1st st to form ring.

Rnd 1: 3 sc in 1st st, 2 sc in next 2 sts, 3 sc in next st, 2 sc in next 2 sts.

Rnd 2: 1 sc in ea st. End off.

Ears

With black yarn, ch 3.

Row 1: 1 sc in 2nd ch from hook, 1 sc in next st, ch 1, turn.

Row 2: 1 sc in next 2 sts, ch 1, turn.

Repeat Row 2 until 9 rows complete, ch 1.

Work 1 row of sc around entire edge to finish off. End off. Make two ears.

BODY

With camel yarn, work the same as head for 1st 4 rnds. Work even on 24 sc until 12 rnds complete.

Rnd 13: Same as Rnd 10 for head.

Rnd 14: Same as Rnd 11 of head.

Stuffing

Insert fiberfill through opening and stuff firmly, molding into a body shape. Finish body by working dec until opening is completely closed. End off by cutting yarn and pulling through last st. Weave end through and trim.

LEGS

With camel yarn, ch 7, sl to 1st ch to form ring.

Rnd 1: 1 sc in ea st (6 sc).

Work even on 6 sc until 8 rnds complete.

Rnd 9: 1 sc in 1st 4 sts, ch 1, turn.

Row 10: 1 sc in 2nd st, 1 sc in next 2 sts. End off. Make four legs.

Soles

Ch 3, sl to 1st st to form ring.

Rnd 1: 6 sc in center of ring, sl to 1st st. End off. Sl sole to leg. Make four soles.

TAIL

With black yarn, ch 15. End off.

Assembling

Sew ears and snout to head. With black embroidery floss, sew nose at tip of snout. With blue embroidery floss, sew eyes above snout and dot with black French knots. Sew legs and tail to body.

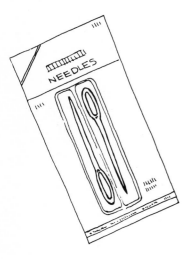

FaIRYTaLe PRINCess

COLOR PLATE 4

Make the **basic doll.**

Hair style/Regular with a top knot using golden brown embroidery
floss.
Take 8 strands of embroidery floss about 6 inches long to match color
of hair and twist tightly together. Tie both ends. Fasten one end of
twist to top of head and wind the twist around in a circle, tucking
the other end under. Pin the bun in place as you go, then tack
securely to head with sewing needle and one strand of embroidery
floss. Make sure to tack down securely at several points so top knot
will not unravel or unwind. (Illustration 34)

ILLUSTRATION 34

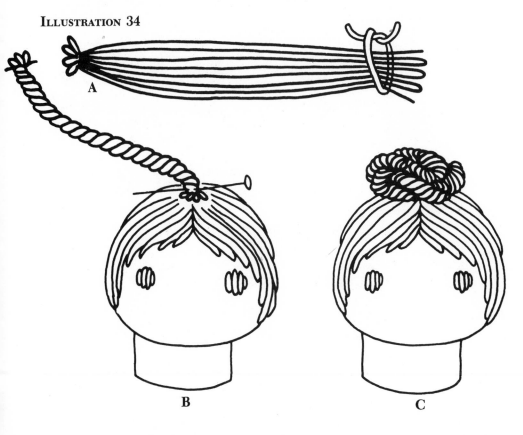

A

B

C

Costume/Halter top and Skirt, Cape, and Crown

Materials:
 Sock and sweater yarn in white
 Metallic gold yarn
 Gold lamé thread
 White angora yarn
 Steel crochet hook, size #2
 Snaps, size 000
 White mercerized cotton thread
 Steel crochet hook, size #7

Gauge:
 6 sts = 1 inch
 7 rows = 1 inch

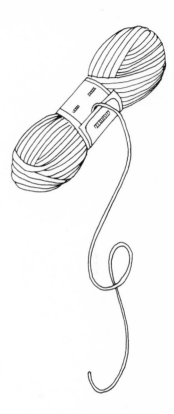

HALTER TOP
With gold yarn, ch 26.
Row 1: 1 sc in 2nd ch from hook and ea st of ch (25 sc), ch 1, turn.
Row 2: Sl 1st st, 1 sc in next 23 sts, turn.
Row 3: ° Sl 1st st, work 1 sc in ea st, sl last st, turn °.
Repeat bet ° of Row 3 until 10 rows complete. End off.

Tie
Attach gold yarn to bottom of left side of halter and work 1 row of sc to finish edge. Work up to 1st st of top row and then ch 20. End off. Work a slip knot in the end and trim.
With gold yarn, ch 20. Attach end of ch to last st of top row of halter and work 1 row of sc down right side, ending off at the bottom.

SKIRT
Attach white yarn to right corner of halter bottom, ch 3.
Row 1: (Ch 3 counts as 1st dc), 1 dc in base of ch 3, 2 dc in ea st across (50 dc) to join sl to top of ch 3. Do not end off. Drop white yarn and pick up gold, ch 1.
Row 2: 1 sc in ea st of row, sl to top of ch 1 but do not end off.
Row 3: Pick up white yarn, ch 3, 1 dc in 2nd st, 2 dc in next st, ° 1 dc in next 2 sts, 2 dc in next st °. Repeat bet ° to end of row, sl to top of ch 3, drop white yarn and pick up gold, ch 1.
Repeat Rows 2 and 3 four more times.
Row 11: With white yarn, 1 dc in ea st, sl to top of ch 3.
Row 12: With gold yarn, 1 sc in 1st st, ch 2, ° 1 sc in next st, ch 2 °. Repeat bet ° to end of row. End off.

CAPE

With white angora yarn, ch 17.

Row 1: 1 sc in 2nd ch from hook and ea st of ch (16 sc), ch 3, turn.

Row 2: 1 dc in base of ch 3, 2 dc in ea st across (32 dc), ch 1, turn.

Row 3: 1 sc in ea dc, ch 1, turn.

Row 4: 1 dc in same st as ch 3, ° 1 sc in next st, 2 dc in next st °. Repeat bet ° to end of row. End off.

Collar

Attach yarn to top of right side, ch 3, turn.

Row 1: 1 dc in base of ch 3, 2 dc in next 2 sts, 1 dc in next 10 sts, 2 dc in next 3 sts. End off.

CROWN

With gold lamé thread and a #7 steel crochet hook, ch 25, sl to 1st ch to form ring.

Rnd 1: ° 1 sc in next 4 ch (1 sc, 1 dc, ch 3, sl to base of ch 3, 1 dc, 1 sc) in next ch °. Repeat bet ° four more times. End off.

The crown fits around the top knot of hair.

7
An Assortment for Holidays

These seasonal dolls are designed to give a new look to your decorations for parties and holiday festivities. They make thoughtful gifts for friends and family and can be used as package ornaments, too. Or keep the dolls from year to year as part of your family's traditional celebration.

Santa and his tree will see many a Christmas season . . .
on the table or as ornaments on your tree.

The bunny and chick celebrate Easter or May Day or any
lovely spring day. Wear the daffodil on your coat collar until the
first real daffodils emerge in the early spring.

The witch and pumpkin can decorate a Halloween table, serve as party favors, or delight a special friend.

The mushroom makes the miniature elf seem even more minute. You might like to make an elf to join Santa and his tree for an elaborate Christmas scene. A group of elves would be appropriate for St. Patrick's Day celebrations too.

santa

COLOR PLATE 6

Make the **basic doll.**

Hair style/Regular with white yarn.

Sew hair in the regular manner but make the front resemble bangs by leaving 1 row of sc bet the hair and eyes. Use red embroidery floss for sewing the nose and black for the eyes. Sew the nose 1 row down from the eyes. Using white yarn, sew a mustache from lower end of the nose to the side of the face slightly below nose. For beard, use white yarn doubled. Pull yarn through chin area 1 sc at a time. Cut yarn, leaving beard about 3 inches long. When entire chin area is covered, trim beard so it is slightly longer in front and tapers toward sides. (Illustration 35)

ILLUSTRATION 35

Costume/Jacket, Pants, Boots, Belt, and Hat

Materials:
  Sock and sweater yarn in red, white, and black
  White angora yarn
  Steel crochet hook, size #2
  Small buckle
  Snaps, size 000
  White and black mercerized cotton thread

Gauge:
  6 sts = 1 inch
  7 rows = 1 inch

JACKET
With red yarn, ch 17.
Row 1: 1 sc in 2nd ch from hook and in ea ch (16 sc), ch 1, turn.
Row 2: 2 sc in ea st across (32 sc), ch 1, turn.
Row 3: 1 sc in 1st 5 sts, ch 5, sk 5 sts, 1 sc in next 12 sts, ch 5, sk 5 sts, 1 sc in last 5 sc, ch 1, turn.
Row 4: 1 sc in ea st across, picking up 5 sc in ea ch 5, ch 1, turn.
Row 5: 1 sc in ea st across (32 sc), ch 1, turn.
Repeat Row 5 sixteen more times. End off.

Sleeves
Attach yarn at underarm and pick up 12 sc around armhole.
Work even on 12 sc for 12 rnds. End off. Make two sleeves.

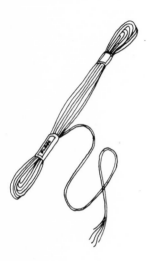

Fur trim
Attach white angora yarn at center back and work 1 row of sc around entire jacket, sl to 1st st. Working from left to right, work 1 row of back sc in ea st, sl to 1st st. End off.
Close jacket front with snaps. Work fur trim around sleeves as well.

PANTS
With red yarn, ch 24, sl to 1st ch to form ring.
Rnd 1: 1 sc in ea st (24 sc).
Rnd 2: Work even on 24 sc until 6 rnds complete.

Right leg
Ch 4, sk 12 sts, attach ch to 13th st, 1 sc in ea st, pick up 4 sc in ch 4. Continue to work even on 16 sc until 13 rnds complete.
Rnd 14: Work dec, 1 sc in next 8 sts, 1 dec, work to end of rnd. End off.

Left leg
Attach yarn at back of pants and work left leg to correspond to right.

BOOTS
With black yarn, ch 12, sl to 1st st to form ring.
Rnd 1: 1 sc in ea ch (12 sc).

112

Rnd 2: Work even on 12 sc until 6 rnds complete.

Row 7: Work 6 sc, ch 1, turn.

Row 8: 1 sc in 2nd st, 1 sc in next 4 sts, ch 1, turn.

Row 9: 1 sc in 2nd st, 1 sc in next 3 sts. End off.

Add fur trim as for the jacket. Make two boots.

Sole

With black yarn, ch 4, sl to 1st ch to form ring.

Rnd 1: 6 sc in center of ring.

Rnd 2: 3 sc in 1st st, 2 sc in next 2 sts, 3 sc in next st, 2 sc in next 2 sts, sl to next st.

Rnd 3: 1 sc in next st, 3 sc in next st, 1 sc in next 5 sts, 3 sc in next st, 1 sc in next 5 sts, sl to next st. Sl st the sole to bottom of the boot. Make two soles.

BELT

With black yarn, ch 3, 1 sc in 2nd ch from hook and in last ch, ch 1, turn.

Row 2: 1 sc in next 2 sts, ch 1, turn.

Repeat Row 2 until belt measures 8 inches. End off.

A small buckle, from an old watch band perhaps, can be sewn on the belt.

HAT

With red yarn, ch 25, sl to 1st ch to form ring.

Rnd 1: 1 sc in ea st (25 sc).

Rnd 2: ° 1 sc in next 6 sts, work dec, °. Repeat bet ° until 12 rnds complete. Continue to dec every st until 1 loop left. End off.

Work fur trim around bottom of hat and add small pompom to the top.

CHRISTMAS TREE

COLOR PLATE 6

Materials:
>   Sock and sweater yarn in green
>   Steel crochet hook, size #2
>   Polyester fiberfill
>   Gold beads
>   Green mercerized cotton thread
>   Bead needle

Gauge:
>   6 sts = 1 inch
>   7 rows = 1 inch

TREE CONE

With green yarn, ch 48, sl to 1st st to form ring, ch 1.

Rnd 1: 1 sc in ea st of rnd (48 sc), sl to top of ch 1, ch 3.

Rnd 2: ° 1 dc in next 5 sts [work dec as follows: yo hook, insert into 1st st, yo and pull up a loop, yo and pull a loop through 2 loops on hook (2 loops remaining on hook), yo hook, insert into 2nd st, and pull loop through, yo and pull a loop through 2 loops on hook (3 loops remaining on hook), yo and pull a loop through all 3 loops on hook] °. Repeat bet ° to end of rnd.

Rnd 3: 1 sc in ea st of rnd below, sl to top of ch 1, ch 3.

Repeat Rnds 2 and 3 nine more times. End off.

Note: Some rnds will not come out even; there will be more or less than 5 sts after last dec. This does not matter.

BRANCHES

° Attach yarn at beg of Rnd 3, working through entire sc, work 4 dc in ea st of rnd, sl to top of ch 3. End off. ° Repeat bet ° on very rnd of sc in bet the rnds of dc.

TOP

Ch 4, sl to 1st ch to form ring.

Rnd 1: Ch 3, 5 dc in 1st st, 6 sc in remaining sts of ch, sl to top of ch 3.

Place this piece on top of tree and tack in place.

115

BASE

Ch 4, sl to 1st ch to form ring.

Rnd 1: Ch 3 (counts as 1st dc), 11 dc in center of ring, sl to top of ch 3, ch 3.

Rnd 2: 1 dc in base of ch 3, 2 dc in ea st of rnd, sl to top of ch 3 (24 dc).

Rnd 3: ° 2 dc in next st, 1 dc in next st °. Repeat bet ° to end of rnd, sl to top of ch 3 (36 dc), ch 3.

Rnd 4: 1 dc in next st, ° 2 dc in next st, 1 dc in next st, 1 dc in next 2 sts °. Repeat bet ° to end of rnd (48 dc), sl to top of ch 3. End off. Place base to tree through top loops only. End off.

Assembly

Place base at bottom of cone. Sl st tog through top loops only. Leave 3 inches open for stuffing.

Stuffing

Insert fiberfill through opening and stuff tree firmly. Finish closing the last 3 inches. End off. Weave end through and trim. Sew beads randomly on tree for ornaments.

BUNNY

COLOR PLATE 7

Materials:

   White and pink angora yarn
   Steel crochet hook, size #2
   Embroidery floss in blue, black, and pink
   Embroidery needle
   Polyester fiberfill
   White mercerized cotton thread

NOTE: This rabbit has been made with angora yarn which works up slightly larger in scale than the sock and sweater yarn. If you prefer, the thinner yarn can be used.

HEAD

With white yarn, ch 4, sl to 1st ch to form ring.

Rnd 1: 6 sc in center of ring.

Rnd 2: 2 sc in ea st (12 sc).

Rnd 3: ° 1 sc in next st, 2 sc in next st °. Repeat bet ° to end of rnd (18 sc).

Rnd 4: ° 1 sc in next 2 sts, 2 sc in next st °. Repeat bet ° to end of rnd (24 sc).

Rnd 5: Work even on 24 sc until 9 rnds complete.

Rnd 10: ° 1 sc in next 2 sts [insert hook into next st and pull yarn through; keeping yarn on hook, insert into next st, yo hook and through all 3 loops (dec made)] °. Repeat bet ° to end of rnd.

Rnd 11: ° 1 sc in next st, (dec) next 2 sts °. Repeat bet ° to end of rnd.

Stuffing

Insert fiberfill through opening and stuff firmly, making head as round as possible. Finish head by working dec until opening is completely closed. End off by cutting yarn and pulling through last st. Weave end through and trim.

Ears

With pink yarn, ch 3, 1 sc in 2nd ch from hook, 1 sc in last st, ch 1, turn.

Row 2: 1 sc in ea st (2 sc), ch 1, turn.

Repeat Row 2 until 8 rows complete, ch 1, turn, 1 sc in last st. End off.

Attach white angora yarn to lower right side and work 1 row of sc around to left corner. Make two ears.

BODY

Work the same as head for 1st 4 rnds.

Work even on 24 sc until 15 rnds complete.

Rnd 16: Same as Rnd 10 of head.

Rnd 17: Same as Rnd 11 of head.

Stuffing

Insert fiberfill through opening and stuff firmly, molding into body shape. Finish body by working dec until opening is completely closed. End off by cutting yarn and pulling through last st. Weave end through and trim.

118

FRONT LEGS

Ch 8, sl to 1st ch to form ring.

Rnd 1: 1 sc in ea st of ch (8 sc).

Rnd 2: Work 1 sc in ea st and continue until 12 rnds complete.

Rnd 13: Work dec until completely closed, pull yarn through last loop, secure and pull end to the inside. Make two front legs and stuff loosely.

BACK LEGS

Ch 11.

Rnd 1: 1 sc in 2nd ch from hook and in next 8 ch, 3 sc in last ch. Working on opposite side of ch, 1 sc in next 8 sts, 2 sc in last st. End off.

Make four pieces. Holding wrong sides tog, sl st 2 pieces tog through back loops only.

Assembling

Sew ears to top of head. Sew eyes with blue embroidery floss, adding a French knot at lower edge of eye in black. Sew nose with pink embroidery floss. Sew front legs 2 rnds below head directly at sides of body. Sew back legs to bottom of body, angling heels in at the back and toes slightly outward.

DaFFODIL

COLOR PLATES 7 AND 9

Materials:

    Sock and sweater yarn in orange, yellow, and green

    Steel crochet hook, size #2

    Stem wire

Gauge:

    6 sts = 1 inch

    7 rows = 1 inch

CENTER

With orange yarn, ch 4, sl to 1st st to form ring.

Rnd 1: 6 sc in center of ring.

Rnd 2: 2 sc in ea st (12 sc), sl to next st, ch 2.

Rnd 3: ° sk 1 st, sl to next st (through bottom loop only), ch 2 °. Repeat bet ° five more times, sl to 1st st.

Rnd 4: Holding Rnd 3 forward with thumb, 1 sc in ea top loop of Rnd 2.

Rnd 5: Work even on 12 sc for 4 more rnds.

Rnd 9: ° ch 3, sl to next st °. Repeat bet ° to end of rnd. Sl to 1st st. End off.

PETALS

With yellow yarn, attach to a ch 2 space in Rnd 3, ch 3.

Row 1: 3 dc in ch 2 space, ch 1, turn.

Row 2: 1 sc in 1st 3 sts, 2 sc in top of ch 3 (5 sc), ch 1, turn.

Row 3: 1 sc in ea st, ch 1, turn.

Row 4: Repeat Row 3 five more times, ch 1, turn.

Row 9: Sk 1st st, 1 sc in next 4 sts, ch 1, turn.

Row 10: Sk 1st st, 1 sc in next 3 sts, ch 1, turn.

Row 11: Sk 1st st, 1 sc in next 2 sts, ch 1, turn.

Row 12: Sk 1st st, 1 sc in next st, pull end through last loop. End Off.

STEM

With green yarn, ch 4.

Rnd 1: Working through top loop of ch, 1 sc in ea st (4 sc). Continue working 1 sc in top loop of sc below. This will form a tube. Work rnds until stem measures 4 inches but do not end off. Ch 15, ° 1 sc in 2nd ch from hook, 1 hdc in next 2 ch, 1 dc in next 2 ch, 1 tr in next 2 ch, 1 dc in next 2 ch, 1 hdc in next 2 ch, 1 sc in next 2 ch, °. Sl to top of stem, ch 15. Repeat bet °. End off.

Assembling

Slip a stem wire up through stem tube and attach to flower between petals. You may want to press the petals flat.

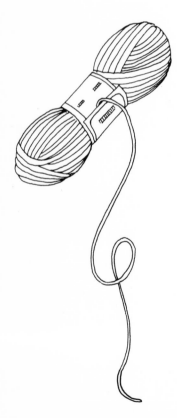

120

CHICK

COLOR PLATE 7

Materials:

> Yellow and orange fluffy yarn
> Steel crochet hook, size #2
> Black embroidery floss
> Embroidery needle
> Polyester fiberfill
> Yellow mercerized cotton thread

NOTE: This chick has been made with fluffy yarn similar in weight to angora. This yarn works up slightly larger in scale than the sock and sweater yarn. Angora or mohair yarn are other alternatives. If you prefer, thinner yarn can be used.

HEAD

With yellow yarn, ch 4, sl to 1st ch to form ring.

Rnd 1: 6 sc in center of ring. Place marker to indicate beg of rnd.

Rnd 2: 2 sc in ea st (12 sc).

Rnd 3: ° 1 sc in next st, 2 sc in next st °. Repeat bet ° to end of rnd (18 sc).

Rnd 4: ° 1 sc in next 2 sts, 2 sc in next st °. Repeat bet ° to end of rnd (24 sc).

Rnd 5: Work even on 24 sc until 9 rnds complete.

Rnd 10: ° 1 sc in next 2 sts [insert hook into next st and pull yarn through; keeping yarn on hook, insert hook into next st, yo hook and through all 3 loops (dec made)] °. Repeat bet ° to end of rnd.

Rnd 11: ° 1 sc in next st, (dec) next 2 sts °. Repeat bet ° to end of rnd.

Stuffing

Insert fiberfill through opening and stuff firmly, making head as round as possible. Finish head by working dec until opening is

121

completely closed. End off by cutting yarn and pulling through last st. Weave end through and trim.

BEAK
With orange yarn, ch 3.
Row 1: 1 sc in 2nd st, 1 sc in next st, ch 1, turn.
Row 2: 1 sc in ea st across (2 sc), ch 1, turn.
Repeat Row 2 one more time.
Row 4: 1 sc in last st. End off.

BODY
Work the same as head for last 4 rnds. Work even on 24 sc until 12 rnds complete.
Rnd 13: Same as Rnd 10 of head.
Rnd 14: Same as Rnd 11 of head.

Stuffing
Insert fiberfill through opening and stuff firmly, molding into a body shape. Finish body by working dec until opening is completely closed. End off by cutting yarn and pulling through last st. Weave end through and trim.

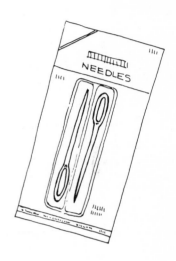

WINGS
Row 1: Ch 5, 1 sc in 2nd st, 1 sc in next 3 sts, ch 1, turn.
Row 2: 1 sc in ea st (4 sc), ch 1, turn.
Repeat Row 2 until 6 rows complete.
Row 7: 1 sc in 2nd st, 1 sc in next 2 sts.
Row 8: 1 sc in 2nd st, 1 sc in next st. End off.
Attach yarn in 1st row and work 1 row of sc around edge to finish off. Make two wings.

FEET
With orange yarn, ch 4.
Row 1: 1 sc in 2nd st, 1 sc in next 2 sts, ch 1, turn.
Row 2: 1 sc in ea st (3 sc), ch 3, sl to 1st st, ch 3, sl to next st, ch 3, sl to last st. End off. Make two feet.

Assembling
Attach orange yarn to 1st row of beak and repeat from Row 1 to end. Fold beak in half and tack to head. Sew eyes in black embroidery floss. Attach wings to side of body and feet to bottom.

123

WANDA THE WITCH

COLOR PLATE 8

Make the **basic doll.**
Hair style/Regular with orange embroidery floss.

Costume/Dress and Hat

Materials:
    Sock and sweater yarn in black
    Steel crochet hook, size #2
    Snaps, size 000
    Black mercerized cotton thread
Gauge:
    6 sts = 1 inch
    7 rows = 1 inch

DRESS
With black yarn, ch 17.
Row 1: 1 sc in 2nd st from hook, and ea st of ch (16 sc), ch 1, turn.
Row 2: 2 sc in ea st across (32 sc), ch 1, turn.
Row 3: 1 sc in 1st 5 sts, ch 5, sk 5 sts, 1 sc in next 12 sts, ch 5, sk 5 sts, 1 sc in last 5 sts, ch 1, turn.
Row 4: 1 sc in ea st across, picking up 5 sc in ea ch 5, ch 1, turn.
Row 5: 1 sc in ea st across, ch 1, turn.
Repeat Row 5 five more times, ch 3, turn.
Row 11: 2 dc in ea st across (64 dc), ch 3, turn.
Row 12: 1 dc in ea st across, ch 3, turn.
Row 13: 1 dc at base of ch 3, 1 dc in ea st across, ch 3, turn.
Row 14: ° 1 dc in next 6 sts, 2 dc in next st °. Repeat bet ° to end of row, ch 3, turn.
Row 15: 1 dc in ea st across, ch 3, turn.
Repeat Row 15 five more times.
Finish bottom with 1 row of sc. End off.
Sew to below waist, close back with snaps.

Sleeves

Attach yarn at underarm and ch 3, pick up 14 dc evenly spaced around armhole, sl to top of ch 3, ch 3, turn.

Row 2: 1 dc in ea st, inc by adding 1 dc in center st at underarm.

Repeat Row 2 until 5 rows complete. Make two sleeves.

Collar

Attach yarn at right side of neck edge, ° ch 3, work 2 dc in 1st 8 sts, ch 1, turn.

Row 2: 1 sc in ea st. End off °.

Attach yarn in 9th st of left side of neck edge. Repeat bet °.

HAT

With black yarn, ch 25, sl to 1st ch to form ring.

Rnd 1: 1 sc in ea st (25 sc).

Rnd 2: ° 1 sc in next 7 sts, work dec °.

Repeat bet ° until 12 rnds complete.

Rnd 13: Work dec until 1 loop remains. End off. Pull yarn through loop and secure, pulling end through to inside of hat.

Brim

Attach yarn to bottom edge of hat and ch 3, 1 dc in base of ch 3, 2 dc in ea st, sl to top of ch 3, ch 1.

Row 2: 1 sc in ea st, sl to top of ch 1. End off.

PUMPKIN

COLOR PLATE 8

Materials:

    Sock and sweater yarn in orange and brown
    Steel crochet hook, size #2
    Tapestry needle, size #18
    Polyester fiberfill

126

Gauge:

    6 sts = 1 inch

    7 rows = 1 inch

PUMPKIN

With orange yarn, ch 4, sl to 1st ch to form ring.

Rnd 1: 6 sc in center of ring.

Rnd 2: 2 sc in ea st (12 sc).

Rnd 3: ° 1 sc in next st, 2 sc in next st °. Repeat bet ° to end of rnd (18 sc).

Rnd 4: ° 1 sc in next 2 sts, 2 sc in next st °. Repeat bet ° to end of rnd (24 sc).

Rnd 5: ° 1 sc in next 3 sts, 2 sc in next st °. Repeat bet ° to end of rnd (30 sc).

Rnd 6: ° 1 sc in next 4 sts, 2 sc in next st °. Repeat bet ° to end of rnd (36 sc).

Rnd 7: Work even on 36 sc for 4 more rnds.

Rnd 11: ° 1 sc in next 2 sts, dec next 2 sts °. Repeat bet ° to end of rnd.

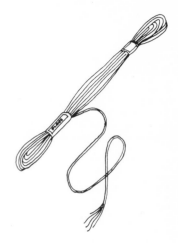

Stuffing

Insert fiberfill through opening and stuff firmly, making pumpkin as round as possible. Finish pumpkin by working dec until opening is completely closed. End off by cutting yarn and pulling through last st. Weave end through and trim.

Assembling

Thread tapestry needle with brown yarn doubled. Make knot in bottom and push needle up through the center. Pull yarn so that ball shape is slightly flattened to resemble a pumpkin shape. Continue to work yarn up through the top center and around back to the bottom center six times, spacing sts equally. Tie off and leave a small end at top to resemble stem.

ELF

COLOR PLATE 9

Since the elf is slightly smaller than the basic doll, the instructions include the entire doll and costume to scale.

Hair style/Regular with brown embroidery floss.

Costume/Jacket, Pants, and Cap

Materials:
> Sock and sweater yarn in pink and green
> Steel crochet hook, size #2
> Polyester fiberfill
> Embroidery floss in black
> Small gold beads
> Small bell
> Pink and green mercerized cotton thread

Gauge:
> 6 sts = 1 inch
> 7 rows = 1 inch

Doll

HEAD
With pink yarn, ch 4, sl to 1st ch to form ring.
Rnd 1: 6 sc in center of ring.
Rnd 2: 2 sc in ea st (12 sc).
Rnd 3: ° 1 sc in next st, 2 sc in next st °. Repeat bet ° to end of rnd (18 sc).
Rnd 4: ° 1 sc in next st [insert hook into next st and pull yarn through; keeping yarn on hook, insert hook into next st, yo hook and through all 3 loops (dec made)] °. Repeat bet ° to end of rnd.

129

Stuffing

Insert fiberfill through opening and stuff firmly, making head as round as possible. Finish head by working dec until opening is completely closed. End off by cutting yarn and pulling through last st. Weave end through and trim.

NECK

Ch 8, sl to 1st ch to form ring.
Rnd 1: 1 sc in ea st (8 sc). Work even on 8 sts until 2 rnds complete. End off.

BODY

Work the same as head for 1st 3 rnds. Work even on 18 sc until 12 rnds complete.
Rnd 13: Same as Rnd 4 for head.

Stuffing

Insert fiberfill through opening and stuff firmly, molding into a body shape. Finish body by working dec until opening is completely closed. End off by cutting yarn and pulling through last st. Weave end through and trim.

ARMS

Ch 7, sl to 1st ch to form ring (7 sc).
Rnd 1: 1 sc in ea st to end of rnd.
Rnd 2: Work even on 7 sc until 11 rnds complete. Work dec until completely closed. Make two arms.

Stuffing

Stuff arms loosely, using small pieces of fiberfill and poking them through opening with heavy end of crochet hook.

LEGS

Ch 8, sl to 1st st to form ring.
Rnd 1: 1 sc in ea st of ch (8 sc). Continue to work even on 8 sc until 12 rnds complete. Make two legs.

Feet

Work 4 sc, ch 1, turn.
1 sc in 2nd st, 1 sc in next 2 sts. End off. Make two feet.

Soles

Ch 4, sl to 1st ch to form ring.
Rnd 1: 8 sc in center of ring. Make two soles.

Assembling

Pin sole to bottom of foot flap. Sew or sl st sole to bottom of foot and leg. End off.

Stuffing

Insert small pieces of fiberfill through opening. Work stuffing into foot with heavy end of crochet hook. Unlike arms, make the legs firm.

For instructions on sewing together, embroidering the features, and making hair, see page 33.

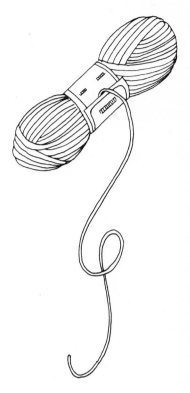

Elf Costume

JACKET
With green yarn, ch 15.
Row 1: 1 sc in 2nd ch from hook and ea st of ch (14 sc), ch 1, turn.
Row 2: 2 sc in ea st across (28 sc), ch 1, turn.
Row 3: 1 sc in 1st 4 sts, ch 5, sk 5 sts, 1 sc in next 10 sts, ch 5, sk 5 sts, 1 sc in last 4 sts, ch 1, turn.
Row 4: 1 sc in ea st across, picking up 5 sc in ea ch 5, ch 1, turn.
Row 5: 1 sc in ea st across row, ch 1, turn.
Repeat Row 5, working on 28 sc even for 12 more rows. End off.

Sleeves

Pick up 10 sc around armhole and work even until 10 rnds complete. End off. Make two sleeves. Attach yarn to upper left corner of jacket and work 1 row of sc to finish edge, ending in upper right corner. Sew small beads for buttons and close jacket with snaps.

PANTS
With green yarn, ch 18, sl to 1st st to form ring.
Rnd 1: 1 sc in ea st (18 sc).
Rnd 2: Work even on 18 sc until 4 rnds complete, ch 3.

Right leg

Sk 9 sc, attach ch to 10th st, work 9 sc, pick up 3 sc in ch 3. Work even on 12 sc until 12 rnds complete. End off.

Left leg

Attach yarn at center back of pants and work left leg to correspond to right.

CAP

With green yarn, ch 18, sl to 1st st to form ring.
Rnd 1: 1 sc in ea st (18 sc).
Rnd 2: ° 1 sc in 1st 5 sts, work dec °. Repeat bet ° until 10 rnds complete. Sl yarn through opening which is now very small and close. End off. Reach crochet hook up through cap from inside and pull end through.
Sew small bell to tip of cap.

MUSHROOM

COLOR PLATE 9

Materials:

Sock and sweater yarn in camel and brown
Steel crochet hook, size #2
Polyester fiberfill

Gauge:

6 sts = 1 inch
7 rows = 1 inch

STEM

With brown yarn, ch 4, sl to 1st ch to form ring.
Rnd 1: 6 sc in center of ring.
Rnd 2: 2 sc in ea st (12 sc).
Rnd 3: ° 1 sc in next st, 2 sc in next st °. Repeat bet ° to end of rnd (18 sc).
Rnd 4: ° 1 sc in next 2 sts, 2 sc in next st °. Repeat bet ° to end of rnd (24 sc).

132

COLOR PLATE 5
Richie (page 92) and Champ (page 95)

COLOR PLATE 6
Santa (page 111) and the Christmas Tree (page 115)

COLOR PLATE 7
Bunny (page 116) with Daffodil (page 119); Flower Hill (page 164); and Chick
(page 121)

COLOR PLATE 8
Wanda (page 125) and Pumpkin (page 126)

COLOR PLATE 9
Elf (page 129) with Mushroom (page 132); Flower Umbrella (page 85); and
Daffodil (page 119)

COLOR PLATE 10
Anna (page 147) and Flower Hill (page 164)

COLOR PLATE 11
Clarence (page 148)

COLOR PLATE 12
Bride (page 153); Groom (page 157); and Silver Bells (page 162)

Rnd 5: ° 1 sc in next 3 sts, 2 sc in next st °. Repeat bet ° to end of rnd (30 sc).

Rnd 6: Place marker to indicate beg of rnd. Work even on 30 sc for 24 more rnds.

End off.

CAP BASE

Rnd 30: Attach camel yarn, ch 3, 1 dc at base of ch 3, 2 dc in ea st of rnd (60 dc), sl to top of ch 3, ch 3.

Rnd 31: 1 dc in next 4 sts, 2 dc in next st °, 1 dc in next 5 sts, 2 dc in next st °. Repeat bet ° to end of rnd (70 dc), sl to top of ch 3, ch 3.

Rnd 32: 1 dc in next 4 sts, 2 dc in next st, ° 1 dc in next 5 sts, 2 dc in next st °. Repeat bet ° to end of rnd (84 sc), sl to top of ch 3, ch 1.

Rnd 33: 2 sc in 1st st, 1 sc in next 42 sts, 2 sc in next st, 1 sc in last 41 sts (86 sc). End off.

On Rnd 6 at marker, work 1 rnd of sc, working through entire st. End off. Stuff base firmly with fiberfill.

CAP

With camel yarn, ch 4, sl to 1st st to form ring.

Rnd 1: 6 sc in center of ring.

Rnd 2: 2 sc in ea st to end of rnd (12 sc).

Rnd 3: ° 1 sc in next st, 2 sc in next st °. Repeat bet ° to end of rnd (18 sc).

Rnd 4: ° 1 sc in next 2 sts, 2 sc in next st °. Repeat bet ° to end of rnd (24 sc).

Continue to inc ea rnd as follows:

Rnd 5: ° 1 sc in next 3 sts, 2 sc in next st °. Repeat bet ° to end of rnd.

Next rnd 4 sts before inc, next rnd 5 sts before inc. Continue this method until Rnd 14 where there will be 12 sts before inc, making 86 sc.

Rnd 15: Continue to work even on 86 sc for 6 more rnds.

Assembling

Holding cap to base, sl tog through top loops only. When the opening measures about 2 inches, stuff cap with fiberfill and finish closing. End off.

142

8
More for Gift Giving and Decorating

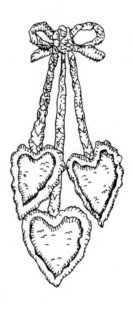

Any item in this book would make an ideal gift, but this chapter is especially dedicated to gift giving and decorating. A homemade gift means you are sharing part of yourself and is a heartfelt way to express your feelings.

And what child would not welcome a birthday party with a ballerina or clown to help celebrate the festive occasion! There are hundreds of uses for these charming holiday characters, so let your imagination be your guide.

The little bridal pair topping off the cake would be a unique addition to any wedding. They will be a welcome part of each anniversary celebration to come as well. The bride and groom would also make a special shower gift or table decoration. To complete the wedding scene, dress a couple of dolls in Southern Belle gowns to serve as bridesmaids.

The wedding decorations might also include the silver bells, on the cake or as part of a gift wrap. They could be used as well as decorations for a 25th anniversary party, a very special occasion indeed.

The hill of flowers can be used alone, perhaps filled with a potpourri of dried flowers to create a pleasant scented atmosphere. Or use it with any of the dolls to create a background and add further dimension to the grouping. The hearts make endearing decorations for a favorite Valentine's gift. They too can be filled with potpourri to be used as a sachet in closets and drawers.

ANNA THE BALLERINA

COLOR PLATE 10

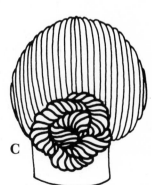

Make the **basic doll** except make the soles of the feet in the same bright pink as the costume and sew or slip stitch to the foot with the same bright pink. Make 2 separate chains of 50 sts each; attach the center of the chain to the center back of the foot. Cross the chain over the center front of the foot and tie in a bow at the back.

Hair style/Regular with a bun using black embroidery floss.
Take 8 strands of embroidery floss about 6 inches long in a color to match the hair and twist tightly together. Tie both ends. Fasten one end of twist to back of head just above the neck and wind the twist around in a circle, tucking the other end under. Pin the bun in place as you go, then tack securely to head with sewing needle and one strand of thread. Make sure to tack securely at several points so bun will not unravel or unwind. (Illustration 36)

ILLUSTRATION 36

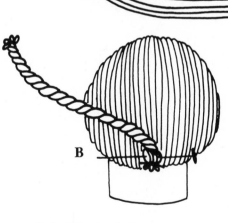

Costume/Tutu and Panties

Materials:
    Sock and sweater yarn in pink
    Steel crochet hook, size #2
    Snaps, size 000
    Pink mercerized cotton thread
Gauge:
    6 sts = 1 inch
    7 rows = 1 inch

TUTU
With pink yarn, ch 27.
Row 1: 1 sc in 2nd ch from hook and ea st of ch (26 sc), ch 1, turn.
Row 2: 1 sc in ea st across, ch 1, turn.
Row 3: Repeat Row 2 until 8 rows complete, ch 4, turn.

Ruffle

Row 9: 3 tr in base of ch 4, 4 tr in ea st across row. End off.
Attach yarn to 1st st of row 8, ch 4, working through entire sc, 3 tr in 1st st, 4 tr in ea st across. End off.

Top

Attach yarn to right side of top and work 1 sc in 1st 3 sts, ch 10, sk 5 sts, 1 sc in next 10 sts, 1 sc in last 3 sts. End off.
Close at back with snaps.

PANTIES

With pink yarn, ch 24, sl to 1st st to form ring.
Rnd 1: 1 sc in ea st (24 sc).
Rnd 2: 1 sc in ea st until 3 rnds complete.
To divide panties and make legs, ch 3, sk 12 sts, 1 sc in next 12 sts, pick up 3 sc in ch 3 (crotch), sl 1 st and continue to work 1 row sc on remaining 12 stitches to make left leg.

Left leg

Attach yarn to center back and work left leg to correspond to right.

CLARENCE THE CLOWN

COLOR PLATE 11

Make the **basic doll** except crochet the entire doll with white yarn. Embroider the face with black and red embroidery floss. See Illustration 37 for stitches.

ILLUSTRATION 37

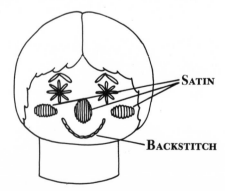

Hair style/Regular with orange embroidery floss.

Costume/Suit, Hat, and Shoes

Materials:

    Sock and sweater yarn in green, yellow, white, and orange
    Steel crochet hook, size #2
    Embroidery floss in black and red
    Embroidery needle
    Snaps, size 000
    Green mercerized cotton thread

Gauge:

    6 sts = 1 inch
    7 rows = 1 inch

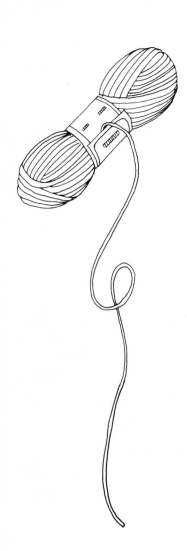

SUIT

With green yarn, ch 17.
Row 1: 1 sc in 2nd ch from hook, and in ea st of ch (16 sc), ch 1, turn.
Row 2: 2 sc in ea st across (32 sc), ch 1, turn.
Row 3: 1 sc in 1st 5 sts, ch 5, sk 5 sts, 1 sc in next 12 sts, ch 5, sk 5 sts, 1 sc in last 5 sts, ch 1, turn.
Row 4: 1 sc in ea st across, picking up 5 sc in ea ch 5, ch 1, turn.
Row 5: 1 sc in ea st across row, ch 1, turn.
Repeat Row 5 thirteen more times, ch 1, turn.
Row 19: 1 sc in 1st 16 sts, ch 4, attach end of ch to 1st st of row. Close at center back with snaps.

Left leg

1 sc in ea st, picking up 4 sc in ch 4.
Work even on 20 sc for 12 rnds.
Rnd 13: Dec in ea st (9 sc). End off.

Right leg

Attach yarn at center back and work right leg to correspond to left.

Sleeves

Attach yarn to armhole and work ° 1 sc in 1st st, 2 sc in next st °.
Repeat bet ° until 15 sc picked up. Work even for 11 rnds.
Rnd 12: Dec 6 times, sl to next st. End off. Make two sleeves.

150

Neck ruffle

Attach yellow yarn to neck edge.

Row 1: Ch 3, 4 dc in 1st st, 5 dc in ea st across neck edge (80 dc). End off.

Sleeve ruffle

Attach yellow yarn to bottom of sleeve, ch 3, 4 dc in 1st st, 5 dc in remaining sts (45 dc), sl to top of ch 3. End off. Repeat for other sleeve.

Leg ruffle

Attach yellow yarn to bottom of leg, ch 3, 4 dc in 1st st, 5 dc in remaining sts (45 dc), sl to top of ch 3. End off. Repeat for other leg.

HAT

With green yarn, ch 26, sl to 1st ch to form ring.

Rnd 1: 1 sc in ea ch (26 sc).

Rnd 2: ° 1 sc in next 5 sts, work dec °. Repeat bet ° to end of rnd.

Rnd 3: ° 1 sc in next 4 sts, work dec °. Repeat bet ° to end of rnd.

Rnd 4: ° 1 sc in next 3 sts, work dec °. Repeat bet ° to end of rnd.

Rnd 5: ° 1 sc in next 2 sts, work dec °. Repeat bet ° to end of rnd.

Rnd 6: 1 sc in next st, work dec until opening is closed.

Attach yellow yarn at bottom of hat, work 4 sc in ea st to end of rnd, sl to 1st st. End off.

Make small pompom in yellow yarn for top of hat.

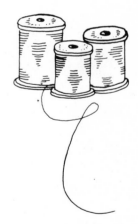

SHOES

With black yarn, ch 4, sl to 1st st to form ring.

Rnd 1: 6 sc in center of ring.

Rnd 2: 3 sc in next st, 2 sc in next 2 sts, 3 sc in next st, 2 sc in next 2 sts.

Rnd 3: 1 sc in next st, 3 sc in next st, 1 sc in next 6 sts, 3 sc in next st, 1 sc in next 6 sts.

Rnd 4: Working in back loop only, work 1 row of sc.

Rnd 5: ° 1 sc in next st, work dec °. Repeat bet ° to end of rnd, sl to next st. End off. Make two shoes.

BRIDE

COLOR PLATE 12

Make the **basic doll.**

Hair style/Regular with wrapped braid using golden embroidery floss.
Take four strands of embroidery floss about 2½ inches long to match color of hair. Twist tightly together. Tie both ends. Fasten each end to the sides of the head. Then, tack securely to head with sewing needle and one strand of embroidery floss. (Illustration 38)

ILLUSTRATION 38

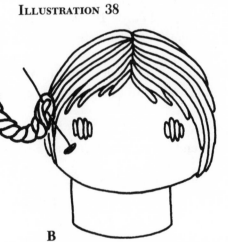

B

C

A

Costume/Dress, Veil and Crown, and Bouquet

Materials:
    Sock and sweater yarn in white
    White cotton crochet thread
    Steel crochet hook, size #2
    Steel crochet hook, size #7
    Miniature white flowers

Gauge:
    6 sts = 1 inch
    7 rows = 1 inch

WEDDING DRESS

With white yarn and a #2 crochet hook, ch 27.

Row 1: 1 sc in 2nd ch from hook and ea st of ch (26 sc), ch 1, turn.

Row 2: 1 sc in ea st across, ch 1, turn.

Repeat Row 2, six more times, ch 3, turn.

Row 9: (1 dc, ch 1, 1 dc) in 2nd st ° (1 dc, ch 1, 1 dc) (shell) in next st °. Repeat bet ° to end of row, ending 1 dc in last st, ch 1, sl to top of ch 3 to join, sl to ch 1 space of 1st shell, ch 4.

Rnd 10: 1 dc in 1st ch 1 space ° (1 dc, ch 2, 1 dc) in next ch 1 space °. Repeat bet ° to end of rnd, sl to top of ch 3, sl to ch 1 space, ch 3.

Rnd 11: 1 dc, ch 1, 2 dc in 1st ch 2 space ° (2 dc, ch 1, 2 dc) in next ch 2 space °. Repeat bet ° to end of rnd, sl to top of ch 3, sl to ch 1 space, ch 4.

Rnd 12: 1 dc in 1st ch 1 space, ch 2 ° (1 dc, ch 2, 1 dc) in next ch 1 space °. Repeat bet ° to end of rnd, sl to top of ch 4, ch 3.

Rnd 13: 1 dc, ch 1, 2 dc in 1st ch 1 space, ° (2 dc, ch 1, 2 dc) in next ch 1 space °. Repeat bet ° to end of rnd, sl to top of ch 3, sl to ch 1 space, ch 5.

Rnd 14: 1 dc in 1st ch 1 space, ch 2 (1 dc, ch 2, 1 dc) in next ch 1 space, ch 2 °. Repeat bet ° to end of rnd, sl to top of ch 3, sl to ch 2 space, ch 3.

Rnd 15: 1 dc, ch 2, 2 dc in ch 2 space ° (2 dc, ch 2, 2 dc) in ch 2 space of next shell °. Repeat bet ° to end of rnd, sl to top of ch 3, sl to next ch 2 space, ch 5.

Rnd 16: 1 dc in ch 2 space of next shell, ch 2 (1 dc, ch 2, 1 dc) in next ch 2 space, ch 2 °. Repeat bet ° to end of rnd, sl to top of ch 3, sl to center of shell, ch 3.

Rnd 17: 1 dc, ch 2, 2 dc in ch 2 space of next shell, ch 1 ° (2 dc, ch 2, 2 dc) in next ch 2 space, ch 1 °. Repeat bet ° to end of rnd, sl to top of ch 3, sl to center of shell, ch 3, sl to base of ch 3 (picot) ° 1 sc in ea dc of shell, 1 sc in ch 1 space, ch 3, sl to base of ch 3 °. Repeat bet ° to end of rnd. End off.

Neck ruffle

Attach yarn at upper right side of dress top.

Row 1: 1 sc in 1st 5 sts, ch 5, sk 5 sts, 1 sc in next 6 sts, ch 5, sk 5 sts, 1 sc in last 5 sts, ch 4, turn.

Row 2: 1 dc in 1st st ° (1 dc, ch 1, 1 dc) (shell) in next st °. Repeat bet ° to end of rnd, working (shell) in ea st of ch 5, ch 1, turn.

Row 3: 1 sc in 3rd st of ch 5, 1 sc in 4th st of ch 5, ch 2, sl to base of ch 2 ° 1 sc in next 2 dc, ch 2, sl to base of ch 2 °. Repeat bet ° to end of row. End off.

Sleeves

Attach yarn at underarm. Pick up 12 sc around armhole edge. Work even until 12 rnds complete.
Rnd 13: Work ° 2 sc in next st, 1 sc in next st °. Repeat bet ° to end of rnd. End off. Make two sleeves.
Sew snaps at back opening.

VEIL

With white cotton crochet thread and #7 crochet hook, ch 40.
Row 1: 1 dc in 4th ch from hook, ch 1, 1 dc in same st ° ch 1, sk 2 ch (1 dc, ch 1, 1 dc) (shell) in 3rd ch, ch 1 °. Repeat bet ° to end of row, ending 1 dc in last ch, ch 4, turn.
Row 2: ° (1 dc, ch 1, 1 dc) in ch 1 space of shell below, ch 1 °. Repeat bet ° to end of row, 1 dc in 3rd st of ch 4 at end of row, ch 4, turn.
Repeat Row 2 fourteen more times, ch 1, turn.
Row 17: ° pull up a loop in next 2 sts, keep loops on hook, yo hook and through all 3 loops (dec made) °. Repeat bet ° to end of row, ch 1, turn.
Row 18: Repeat Row 17, ch 10.
Row 19: Attach end of ch to opposite side of veil. Work 1 row of sc around veil, pick up 1 sc in ea st of ch 10 (20 sc).

Crown

Rnd 20: ° ch 3, sl to base of ch 3, 1 sc in next 4 sts °. Repeat bet ° four more times, sl to 1st st. End off.

BOUQUET

With white yarn and #2 crochet hook, ch 4, sl to 1st st of ch to form ring.
Rnd 1: 8 sc in center of ring, ch 4.
Rnd 2: ° 1 dc, ch 1 °. Repeat bet ° four times in ea st, sl to top of 1st st. End off.
Make a ch of 12. Leave 1½ inches on ea end of ch. Attach one end to a sc of Rnd 1; with the other end, form loop to fit over bride's hand. Slip miniature flowers (or a single flower from the Flower Hill, page 164) through center hole of ring and attach to doll's hand.

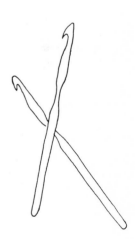

155

GROOM

COLOR PLATE 12

Make the **basic doll.**

Hair style/Regular with light brown embroidery floss.

Costume/Jacket, Pants, Dickey, Tie, and Hat

Materials:
    Sock and sweater yarn in black and white
    Steel Crochet hook, size #2
    Small black beads
    Snaps, size 000
    Black mercerized cotton thread

Gauge:
    6 sts = 1 inch
    7 rows = 1 inch

JACKET

With black yarn, ch 13.

Row 1: 1 sc in 2nd ch from hook and ea st of ch (12 sc), ch 1, turn.

Row 2: 2 sc in ea st across (24 sc), ch 1, turn.

Row 3: 1 sc in 1st st, ch 5, sk 5 sts, 1 sc in next 12 sts, ch 5, sk 5 sts, 1 sc in last st, ch 1, turn.

Row 4: 1 sc in ea st across, picking up 1 sc in ea ch 5, ch 1, turn.

Row 5: 1 sc in ea st across (24 sc), ch 1, turn.

Repeat Row 5 eight more times, ch 1, turn.

Row 14: 2 sc in 1st st, 1 sc in ea st ending 2 sc in last st (26 sc), ch 1, turn.

Row 15: 1 sc in ea st across, ch 1, turn.

Row 16: Repeat Row 14 (28 sc), ch 1, turn.

Row 17: Repeat Row 15 three more times, ch 1, turn.

Row 20: 1 sc in 3rd st, 1 sc in ea st, ending sl to 2nd st from end, ch 1, turn.

Row 21: Repeat Row 20. End off.

157

Lapels

Attach yarn to left edge of Row 15, work 1 row of sc around ending Row 15 of Right side, ch 1, turn.

Row 2: 1 sc in 3rd st, 1 sc in ea st, ending sl to 2nd st from end, ch 1, turn.

Repeat Row 2 one more time. End off.

Attach yarn at center back of jacket, work 1 row of sc around entire jacket including lapels, end at center back, sl to 1st st. End off. Sew beads on front of jacket for buttons. Close jacket front with snap.

PANTS

With black yarn, ch 24, sl to 1st ch to form ring.

Rnd 2: 1 sc in ea ch (24 sc).

Repeat Rnd 2, work even on 24 sc until 8 rnds complete.

Right leg

Ch 3, attach end of ch in 13th st, work 12 sc, pick up 1 sc in ea ch. Work even on 15 sc until 14 rnds complete. End off.

Left leg

Attach yarn at center back and work left leg to correspond to right.

DICKEY

With white yarn, ch 17.

Row 1: 1 sc in 2nd ch from hook and ea st of ch (16 sc), ch 1, turn.

Row 2: 2 sc in ea st across (32 sc), ch 1, turn.

Row 3: 1 sc in 1st 5 sts, ch 5, sk 5 sts, 1 sc in next 12 sts, ch 5, sk 5 sts, 1 sc in last 5 sts. End off.

Row 4: Attach yarn in 1st st to the left of ch 5, work across 12 sc, ch 1, turn.

Row 5: 1 sc in ea st across, 12 sc, ch 1, turn.

Repeat Row 5 until 10 rows complete. End off.

Ties

Ch 25, attach yarn to right front of dickey panel, work 1 sc in ea st across (12 sc), ch 25. End off.

Neck ruffle

Attach yarn to upper right edge of neck, work 3 sc in ea st of neck (48 sc). End off.

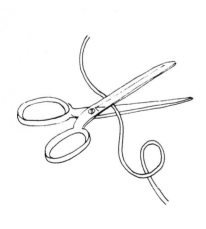

Front ruffle

Ch 10, 4 sc in 2nd ch from hook, 4 sc in ea st of ch, continue working on opposite side of ch with 4 sc in ea st, sl to 1st st. End off.

TIE

With black yarn, ch 10, sl to 1st st, ch 10, sl to 1st st. End off. Tie ends tog tightly, trim.

HAT

With black yarn, ch 4, sl to 1st ch to form ring.

Rnd 1: 12 dc in center of ring.

Rnd 2: * 1 sc in next st, 2 sc in next st *. Repeat bet * to end of rnd (18 sc).

Rnd 3: Working in back loop only, 1 sc in ea st.

Rnd 4: Work even on 18 sc for 5 rnds, ch 2.

Rnd 9: 1 hdc in 1st st, * 2 hdc in next st *. Repeat bet * to end of rnd, sl to 1st st. End off.

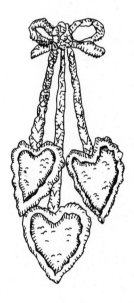

Hearts

Materials:

    Sock and sweater yarn in red and white

    Steel crochet hook, size #2

    Polyester fiberfill

Gauge:

    6 sts = 1 inch

    7 rows = 1 inch

HEART

With red yarn, ch 3.

Row 1: 1 sc in 1st st of ch, ch 1, turn.

Row 2: 3 sc in st below, ch 1, turn.

Row 3: 1 sc in 1st 2 sts, 2 sc in last st, ch 1, turn.

Row 4: Continue to work 1 sc in ea st, 2 sc in last st. This will automatically inc ea row. Repeat this process until there are 12 sc across.

Row 11: Work 1 sc in 1st 6 sts, ch 1, turn.
Row 12: Sk 1st st, 1 sc in next 5 sts, ch 1, turn.
Row 13: Sk 1st st, 1 sc in next 4 sts, ch 1, turn.
Row 14: Sk 1st st, 1 sc in next 3 sts. End off.
Attach yarn in 7th st of Row 11, 1 sc in next 6 sts, ch 1, turn.
Repeat Rows 12 through 14.
Make two pieces.

Assembling

Holding wrong sides together and starting at center top, attach yarn and carefully sl st tog as evenly as possible. When you reach the point at center bottom, ch 3 and continue to sl st tog until opening measures about 1 inch. At this point insert fiberfill, using small pieces and working them around with heavy end of crochet hook. Then close the remaining opening with sl st.

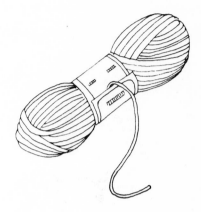

White trim

Attach white yarn at center top, working through top loop only of sl st, ch 4, ° sl to next st, ch 4 °. Repeat bet ° around entire heart. End off. Make 3 hearts.

Ribbons

With white yarn, ch 4.
Row 1: 1 dc in 1st ch, turn, sl to space bet ch 4 and dc.
Row 2: Ch 3, 1 dc, ch 1, 2 dc in space below, turn.
Row 3: ° sl to top of 2nd dc below, sl to ch 1 space, ch 3, 1 dc, ch 1, 2 dc in space °.
Repeat bet ° until piece measures 13 inches. This strip is used as a bow.
Make another strip 7 inches long, one 6 inches, and the third 5 inches. Attach a heart to the bottom of each strip; then place bow at the top of the 3 strips sewn together.

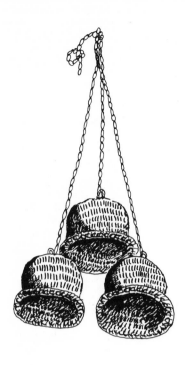

SILVER BELLS

COLOR PLATE 12

Materials:
  Silver lamé elastic thread
  Steel crochet hook, size #7
Gauge:
  9 sts = 1 inch

Ch 4, sl to 1st ch to form ring.
Rnd 1: 6 sc in center of ring.
Rnd 2: 2 sc in ea st (12 sc).
Rnd 3: * 1 sc in next st, 2 sc in next st *. Repeat bet * to end of rnd (18 sc).
Rnd 4: * 1 sc in next 2 sts, 2 sc in next st *. Repeat bet * to end of rnd (24 sc).
Rnd 5: Work even on 24 sc for 5 more rnds.
Rnd 10: * 1 sc in next st, 2 sc in next st *. Repeat bet * to end of rnd.
Rnd 11: 1 sc in ea st. End off. Weave end in carefully as elastic thread is hard to secure and unravels easily.

CLAPPER AND CHAIN
* Ch 55, sl to 3rd st from hook. End off. Weave end into knot and secure well. Insert hook through hole at top of bell and pull chain through until clapper knot is even with the bottom of the bell *. Make a ch of 45 and repeat bet *. Make a ch of 35 and repeat bet *. Tie the ends of the 3 bells tog or use them separately.

FLOWER HILL

COLOR PLATE 7 AND 10

Materials:

Sock and sweater yarn in green, yellow, red, scarlet, tangerine, bright pink, light pink, and light blue.
Steel crochet hook, size #2
Polyester fiberfill
Toothpicks
White household glue

Gauge:

6 sts = 1 inch
7 rows = 1 inch

TOP

With green yarn, ch 4, sl to 1st ch to form ring.
Rnd 1: 6 sc in center of ring.
Rnd 2: 2 sc in ea st (12 sc).
Rnd 3: ° 1 sc in next st, 2 sc in next st °. Repeat bet ° to end of rnd (18 sc).
Rnd 4: ° 1 sc in next 2 sts, 2 sc in next st °. Repeat bet ° to end of rnd (24 sc).
Rnd 5: ° 1 sc in next 3 sts, 2 sc in next st °. Repeat bet ° to end of rnd (30 sc).
Continue separating the increased sts by 1 more st ea rnd until Rnd 14, where there will be 12 sts bet increases (86 sc).
Rnd 15: Work even on 86 sc for 4 more rnds.

BASE

With green yarn, ch 4, sl to 1st ch to form ring, ch 3.
Rnd 1: 11 dc in center of ring (ch 3 counts as dc), sl to top of ch 3, ch 3.
Rnd 2: 2 dc in 2nd st, ° 1 dc in next st, 2 dc in next st °. Repeat bet ° to end of rnd, sl to top of ch 3, ch 3 (24 dc).
Rnd 3: 1 dc in 2nd st, 2 dc in next st, ° 1 dc in next 2 sts, 2 dc in next st °. Repeat bet ° to end of rnd, sl to top of ch 3, ch 3 (36 dc).
Rnd 4: 1 dc in next 2 sts, 2 dc in next st, ° 1 dc in next 3 sts, 2 dc

164

in next st *. Repeat bet * to end of rnd (48 dc).
Rnd 5: 1 dc in next 3 sts, 2 dc in next st, * 1 dc in next 4 sts, 2 dc in next st *. Repeat bet * to end of rnd, sl to top of ch 3, ch 3 (60 dc).
Rnd 6: 1 dc in next 4 sts, 2 dc in next st, * 1 dc in next 5 sts, 2 dc in next st *. Repeat bet * to end of rnd, sl to top of ch 3, ch 3 (72 dc).
Rnd 7: 1 dc in next 5 sts, 2 dc in next st, * 1 dc in next 6 sts, 2 dc in next st *. Repeat bet * to end of rnd, sl to top of ch 3 (84 dc). End off.

Assembling

Hold wrong sides together of the top and base. Sl tog through top loops only. When the opening measures about 2 inches, stuff with fiberfill, then close but do not end off. * Ch 7, sl to next st *. Repeat bet * to end of rnd. End off.

FLOWERS

Center (yellow for all flowers)

With yellow yarn, ch 4, sl to 1st ch to form ring.
Rnd 1: 8 sc in center of ring, sl to 1st st. End off.

Petals

Make two petals each of red, scarlet, tangerine, bright pink, light pink, and light blue.
Attach yarn to 1st sc of center, * 1 sc, 1 dc, 1 tr in 1st st, 1 tr, 1 dc, 1 sc, in next st *. Repeat bet * three more times, sl to 1st st. End off.

Stems

With green yarn, ch 3, sl to 1st ch to form ring.
Rnd 1: Working in top loop only, 1 sc in ea st. Vary the length of the stem from $\frac{1}{2}$ inch to 2 inches. Continue to work 1 sc in ea st until desired length but do not end off.

Leaves

With green yarn, ch 8, * 1 sc in 2nd ch from hook, 1 dc in next 2 sts, 1 tr in next st, 1 dc in next 2 sts, 1 sl st in next st * sl to stem, ch 8. Repeat bet *. End off. Slip a toothpick down through the middle of the stem and insert into mound, placing taller stems on top and shorter ones around bottom edge, as shown. Glue flowers to center of stems between leaves.

166

9
Dolls, Dolls, and More Dolls

In the introduction, I mentioned the idea of using the items in this book as money-making projects. Everywhere I go, I meet people actively engaged in fund raising for charity or other worthy causes. Bazaars and boutique sales of handmade objects are always popular money makers, for which these dolls and decorative items are ideal. Since their creation involves minimal investments of time and money, even a low sale price for a finished project could mean a fine profit.

I take great pleasure, too, in using these dolls to make school studies more visual, more interesting, and more lively. The Dolls From Many Lands in Chapter 5, for example, can illustrate a lesson on traditional native costumes. Displayed against backgrounds that further define their culture, the groups can show how people differ in costume.

There is a doll in this book to illustrate any fairy tale. You could create an entire scene by putting several dolls together. For example, the storybook girl in this chapter could be Snow White; add the witch from Chapter 7 and complete the picture with the elves from Chapter 8. Change the color of the Pilgrim boy's costume and he becomes a prince for the beautiful princess. Once you get into the swing, you will begin to see endless possibilities for storybook character tableaus. After you have created a scene from your favorite story, you can keep the dolls on permanent display in a glass case.

The Dolls With Historical Costumes, Chapter 4, show how Americans have changed clothing styles over their 200-year history. Several dolls dressed like the Pilgrim girl and boy, together with the pumpkin from Chapter 7, could set the stage for a graphic lesson on Thanksgiving. And once these dolls are made, they can remain on permanent display for many successive years of students.

The dolls also take the spotlight during holidays and family celebrations. During the Christmas season, Santa and his tree from Chapter 7, along with the spritely elf in Chapter 8, make a charming decorative scene. Mrs. Claus can be fashioned from the storybook girl in Chapter 6, made with gray hair and wearing a longer dress.

To use any of the projects as Christmas tree ornaments, attach a loop of yarn to the top of the doll's head and hang it from the tree. Think of the effect a whole tree of dolls would make! Of course, these ornaments will last, unbroken and good as new, for generations to come.

Throughout the year the dolls can highlight table centerpieces or home decorations. Brighten the Easter season with a table display featuring the bunny and the chick, Chapter 7, used with colored eggs. The flower hill in Chapter 8, too, makes an excellent spring-time decoration. You might also make several daffodils, featured in Chapter 7, to arrange in a vase, perhaps lengthening the stems for a seasonal floral arrangement.

For friends who collect animals, you can look back through the book to put together a selection. There are the bunny and chick, the dog and the bear (from Chapter 6) all ready to make. The basic body and head structures can be used to create other animals as well. You can make a duck, for example, by crocheting the chick's body in white yarn and holding it lengthwise. Use the instructions for the

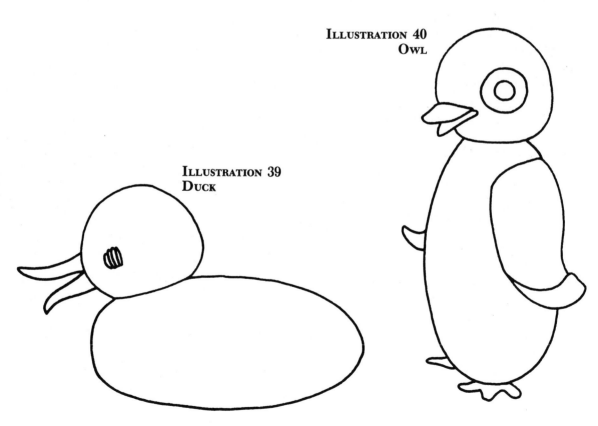

ILLUSTRATION 40
OWL

ILLUSTRATION 39
DUCK

chick's beak but make it slightly larger. (Illustration 39) Or construct an owl with the body, head, and wings of the chick. (Illustration 40) Change the yarn colors, vary the size of the wings, and experiment with owlish eyes made by following the directions for the bear's ears. You can begin to fashion your own creatures once you are familiar with what is in the book and can piece the various parts together in new and exciting ways.

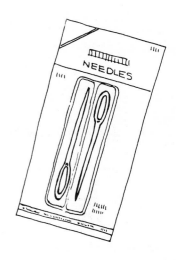

After you have made several different dolls, you might like to try expanding their wardrobes. For example, if you crochet the camel's-hair coat from the Modern Girl's wardrobe in Chapter 4 in brown mohair or angora yarn, it would resemble a fur coat. The princess's dress in Chapter 6 would make an elegant formal gown for the Modern Girl. A jacket without sleeves crocheted in brightly colored stripes would make a high-fashion vest. Pair it with the Eskimo boots from Chapter 5 made taller and without the fur trim. Finish this stylish outfit with a skirt to match the vest. A handsome purse can be fashioned from a small square made of single crochet folded together, with a chain of 25 stitches as a shoulder strap. As you can see, the choices and variations are infinite. A few minor changes in any doll's costume can change the doll entirely. For example, the storybook girl wearing the Pilgrim girl's hat becomes a little Dutch girl. And that, you'll find, is just the beginning!

I have tried to keep the projects in their simplest form to allow for your own creative innovations. I hope that my ideas will stimulate your self-expression and help you to realize that there is creative ability in all of us.

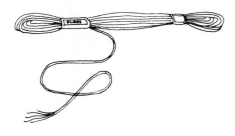

EMBROIDERY STITCH GLOSSARY

Satin Stitch

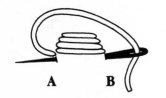

Come up at A and go down at B. Then come up again right next to A and go down again right next to B. Continue coming up on one side of the area to be covered and going down on the other to form a smooth area of stitching.

Back Stitch

Come up at A, go down at B, then up ahead at C. Repeat, going back into same hole that previous stitch began with (A). Keep all stitches the same size.

Chain Stitch Daisy

Bring needle up at A.

Form a loop, and put the needle in at A again, holding loop down with finger. Then come up at B, directly below A. Draw gently through, forming the first chain stitch.

Repeat, always inserting the needle exactly where the thread came out. Rotate the chain stitches to form a flower and secure each chain with a small stitch.

French Knot

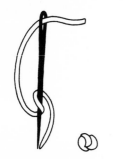

Use embroidery floss doubled. Bring needle up through the fabric to the right side. Wrap thread around the needle closely (but not too tightly). The thread should be wrapped around the needle once to make the neatest knot. Reinsert needle into the fabric next to the thread but not in the exact same spot. Pull needle through.

172